Dancing with Your

Steve Shaw is co-founder of th[...]
he is also a regular speaker. Bas[...] in Cambridge, [...]
Theology at College House and works as a counsellor for the
Caris Counselling Group.

DANCING *with your* SHADOW

Steve Shaw

TRIANGLE

First published 1995
Triangle
SPCK
Holy Trinity Church
Marylebone Road
London
NW1 4DU

The extract from 'Prescience' from *And Still I Rise* by
Maya Angelou is reprinted by kind permission of the publishers,
Virago Press.

British Library Cataloguing-in-Publication Data
A catalogue record for this book is available from the British
Library.

ISBN 0-281-04760-X

Typeset by Dorwyn Ltd, Rowlands Castle, Hants
Printed in Great Britain by BPC Paperbacks Ltd
Member of The British Printing Company Ltd

Contents

Acknowledgements

I would like to thank John Peck, Ruth Edwards, Naomi Starkey and Trisha Dale for reading and commenting on the manuscript. I would also like to thank Carol Holliday for her help and encouragement. I have discussed much of the content of this book with her during the process of its writing and it contains many of her suggestions. Finally, I would like to thank Eric Hutchison, Jungian analyst and Anglican priest. Not only has he taught me much about Jung and the Christian faith, also, with great care, sensitivity and insight, he has helped me to dance with my shadow. I need to say, however, that any nonsense that appears in these pages is my responsibility entirely.

1 *Shadow in the Mist*

'I just don't know what to do.' Martin's face contorted in agony. He was desperate. 'I want to do what God wants, I really do. But . . . .' There was a long pause. 'No sooner do I promise him I'll be better than I just go out and do the same thing again. I'm just bad and that's all there is to it.' Ironically, Martin was beginning to feel a bit better; his face had relaxed a little. Confession always helps, as the Church has known for centuries, but his problem lay a lot deeper: he was emotionally split in two. One part of him he identified as the good boy. The other part he identified as the bad boy. The 'bad boy Martin' was the one who went off with his mates to smoke pot and to play rock and roll music. The 'good boy Martin' was the one who went to church, prayed with all his church friends and promised God that he would never sin again.

The cycle seemed endless. 'Good boy Martin' would go to church, repent and promise to behave. 'Bad boy Martin' would rebel and off he would go and take drugs again. 'Good boy Martin' would be devastated. Yet again he would go to church and repent through tears of anguish. Martin's church friends tried all sorts of ways to help him. 'You're not really accepting God into your life,' they suggested, so intensifying Martin's dilemma by the addition of guilt. Once when Martin came to see me, he had just heard a visiting preacher give a 'prophetic word of knowledge': 'There is someone here in this building who is throwing God's gift of grace back in his face.' Martin groaned. 'I knew he was talking about me,' he said. But the more guilty he felt, it seemed, the more powerfully and irresistibly the bad boy would drive him away again to the 'underworld'.

As a counsellor I felt that I was in a precarious position. When he first came to see me and told me his story I soon sensed that it was 'good boy Martin' who had come. It was a last resort. He wanted me to support him and help him to be good but I knew that if I joined the ranks of the good boy supporters, 'bad boy Martin' would soon appear and take him away. If, on the other hand, I showed any sign of support for 'bad boy Martin', 'good boy Martin' would not respect me. I decided to tell him about 'Jesus the cuddler'.

Jesus was teaching. There was a crowd around him. Some children were pushing forward to get near to him. Jesus' disciples, eager to keep things running smoothly for their great leader, tried to curb the enthusiasm of the children. Jesus, ever open to creative and imaginative opportunities to get his message over, seized his chance for an acted parable. 'Let the children come,' he said defiantly. He took a child in his arms and set the child on his knee. 'This is how you get into the kingdom,' he said, then he cuddled the child (Mark 10.13–16).

I asked, 'Which Martin do you think Jesus would throw his arms around, good Martin or bad Martin?' I held out my arms to emphasize the point that Jesus would throw his arms around 'both Martins'. He nodded. He had got the point, but I wondered if he really believed it.

Martin began to miss some of our weekly sessions. Then his letter came. He thanked me for my help, but circumstances had changed and he felt unable to meet with me any more. I wondered who had written the letter, good Martin or bad Martin. I suspected that it was good Martin. I had given too much support to bad Martin. I wondered if I had been too quick with him. Perhaps I should have been more patient and waited with my stories until both good and bad Martins had gained a little more trust in me.

The great psychologist Carl Gustav Jung used the word 'shadow' to help explain the kind of dilemma Martin faced. The idea came to him in a dream. (It is not so unusual for great discoveries to be inspired by dreams. The chemist Kekule, for example, dreamed of a dancing snake coiling into a circle with its tail in its mouth. This dream image led to the discovery of the benzene ring and the solution to a problem that had been puzzling scientists for some time. We shall talk more of dreams later.) Jung dreamed that he was walking along somewhere at night in a dense fog and against a mighty head wind. He held cupped in his hand a tiny light that threatened to go out at any moment. Suddenly he felt something coming up behind him. He looked round and was terrified to see looming over him a gigantic black figure. When he woke he realized this figure was his own shadow cast by the tiny light on to the swirling mist. As he reflected upon the dream, many hitherto inexplicable personal experiences and inner conflicts began to make sense to him.

Jung went on to develop a profound theory of the structure of the human psyche. Put simply, the small light represents the conscious part of ourselves – the part that loves, hates, feels joy, pleasure and pain, that thinks, believes, makes plans and promises. Many people think that this is all there is to being human. Jung's dream suggested that there is another part to us – a part that lies in a

mysterious mist. It is a part we are not conscious of. It is the unconscious part of ourselves. And here lives, and looms, the shadow.

The dream also told Jung that the unconscious shadow is cast by the light of the conscious mind. Whatever we choose to bring into the light for all to see is that which we approve of in ourselves, or that which we believe others approve of, but there is a price to pay, for when we approve of some things we disapprove of others. It is the things about ourselves that are disapproved of, or that we find threatening, that form our shadow. Martin wanted to identify himself with the 'good boy'. He approved of the one who went to church, felt remorse, repented of his bad behaviour, sought counselling, but the more he tried to live in this light, the greater was the shadow that formed.

We may notice something else about Martin's behaviour. His efforts to live in the light created such a gigantic shadow that it soon overwhelmed him and pushed him into being a 'bad boy'. He then identified with this side of himself for a while. He despised the good boy until the good boy became his shadow and the cycle would begin again. Like most modern writers I am writing this text straight on to a computer. My computer program has a facility called 'windows'. I can split my screen in two sections or windows. If I do not want to use what I have written just now I can transfer it from the operating window to the second window to save it for later. I can flick between window one and window two at the touch of a button. Martin is a little like these windows. Sometimes he is operating in window one as the good boy. Then he flips over into window two and operates as the bad boy. Martin's non-operating window becomes his shadow.

Jung believed that we all have our personal shadows. These may be very different from Martin's shadow but we all have something, or some things, that we wish to hide away, often unconsciously, from other people and also ourselves. Shadows, unfortunately, are not like the windows of computer software. They do not lie idly waiting until we engage them again. If we consistently deny our shadows – if we try to put the lid on them, to change the metaphor, then – like a pressure-cooker, they build up pressure until they explode, spewing out their contents for all to see. No one could have tried harder to hold down his shadow – the bad boy part of himself – than Martin. He had called upon the whole host of heaven to help him yet to no avail; eventually Martin's shadow would burst out again and let him down.

There is another kind of shadow that we also have to face. This we may call the 'collective shadow'. It is the shadow that is cast by communities of people: by companies, institutions, schools, universities, families, work places, offices and nations.[1] Before the Berlin Wall came down, the Soviet Union was saddled with the disowned collective shadow of the West. Westerners saw Russians as 'Satanic conspirators', 'violaters of human rights', 'perpetrators of unspeakable atrocities'. As long as we projected our shadow and found a scapegoat we could carry on thinking that we were righteous. We did not have to own our own violations of human rights and injustices. When the wall came down the disowned collective shadow of the West had to find a new host. It settled on Iraq. We perceived Saddham Hussein as evil incarnate. The shadow of the West is restless again. When our disowned shadow is roaming like this we ought to be nervous. It may settle on someone who will not tolerate the shadow at all. Then all hell could break loose in a war that begins in the shadows.

I live in a city which boasts one of the greatest universities in the world. Some of the most important discoveries about our world have been made here. The list of names of intellectual giants on the chapel wall of just one of the colleges is formidable; so too is the collective shadow.

Some years ago I attended a series of seminars given by an eminent philosopher. I remember when we arrived for the first session how we all gathered in a corridor before a huge oak door. No one spoke. No one tried the door to see if it was unlocked. We just stood there foolishly, held in the grip of a psychic power which seemed to emanate from the centuries-old walls, the floor, the dimly lit corridor, and that huge oak door. Suddenly, what looked like a mad professor appeared from nowhere gesticulating wildly. 'Go in!' shouted the apparition irritatedly, 'Go in!' Obediently, someone pushed on the door. It opened and we felt even more foolish. We went in and sat down. Still none of us spoke. After a while the door swung open. A woman blustered in, went to the front and proceeded to lecture to the wall behind us. She did this once a week for eight weeks – never once making eye contact with any of us. We were a small group – no more than eight. By the end of the series of seminars I had managed to pull myself away a little from the spell we all seemed to be caught in. I rushed out after the lecturer as she was disappearing like a whirlwind up the stairs. I reached out and touched her on the arm to get her attention. She started. It was as if I had violated a centuries-old taboo. I said, 'I want to thank you for your interesting lectures. I have enjoyed them.' She seemed embarrassed by this personal contact and nodded awkwardly before disappearing out of sight.

This story is about the shadow that has been formed over centuries of exaltation of the intellect. It tells of the powerful spell a collective shadow may cast, a spell that had the effect of making us feel like foolish children cowering before a great intellectual parent. The shadow cast by the intellect is composed of other non-intellectual human faculties, particularly the body and the feelings. Sometimes this shadow is very dark indeed. The suppression of the emotions can lead to intense emotional distress.

In some cases it may even be a factor leading to suicide. If you are part of a powerful institution where self-worth is measured solely in terms of intellectual prowess, feelings of worthlessness are not far away.

In this book we will explore the personal shadow. We will also explore the collective shadow, focusing particularly on the shadow cast by the exaltation of the intellect. Looking from both a theological and a psychological perspective we will see how the shadow is formed, how we may discover the shadow, and finally how we may dance with the shadow. Before we begin our shadow work, however, we need to do some groundwork.

2 An Invitation to Dance

This book turns upon some of the central ideas of C. G. Jung. Jung is a controversial figure: some people embrace everything he says as wisdom that demands genuflectional allegiance. Others dismiss him as a charlatan, heretic, racist, male chauvinist and dabbler in the occult. I am aware of most of the serious criticisms of Jung and various aspects of his thought and have reflected upon these. This book, however, is not the place to enter into a detailed critical discussion. I must refer the reader who is interested in this to the bibliography at the end of the book. Having said this, because Jung draws such a powerful, mixed and, in my opinion, often ill-thought-through response I do feel I need to give the reader an orientation to this book.

I believe the problem about Jung raises more general questions. Where is wisdom to be found? How should we recognize it? These are profound questions that are also raised in the Christian Scriptures themselves. A quick answer to such questions would be facile. In the book of Job, facile answers were given by all parties to the discussion. Such responses all incurred the disapproval of God (Job 28.12; 38.1ff., 42.7ff.). The book of Job ought to curb any overenthusiasm concerning claims to knowledge of the nature and whereabouts of wisdom. However, the Scriptures do, I believe, give us some pointers as to where we are to look and how we may recognize wisdom.

The Scriptures assume, of course, that God is the source of wisdom. We meet God in creation itself. When the apostle Paul wrote the following words in his letter to the Christians living in Corinth he was reflecting this theological truth: 'But God, who comforts the downcast, comforted us by the coming of Titus' (2 Cor. 7.6). Paul believed that God's presence was mediated to him through the visit of his friend. This idea of mediated presence is central to biblical religion. It is brought into a sharp focus in the person of Christ but is everywhere present in the Scriptures. It rests on the profound and much neglected doctrine of creation.[1] Because God is the Creator of the world he has, since the beginning, been intimately involved with his creation. In Gen. 3.8 we find God 'walking in the garden [of creation] in the cool of the day'. The Psalmist declares that God 'covers the heavens with clouds, he prepares rain for the earth, he makes grass grow upon the hills. He gives to the beasts their food and to the young ravens which cry' (Ps. 147.8–9). The prophet Isaiah tells us that the hand of God is to be seen in the political contingencies of his day: 'Have you not known? Have you not heard? . . . It is he . . . who brings princes to nought, and makes the rulers of the earth as nothing' (Isa. 40.21–3).

The God of the Bible, then, is a God who makes himself known in and through creation and everything that goes on in creation. An Old Testament scholar put it like this: 'For Israel there was only one world of experience. The experiences of the world were for her always divine experiences as well, and the experiences of God were for her experiences of the world.'[2] Second, it seems that we may find God in the most unlikely or even religiously offensive places. Jesus offended the moral, political and religious sensibilities of the religious people of his day because he 'supped with sinners': he kept company with prostitutes and those who collected taxes for the Roman oppressors. Jesus shows us the God whom we worship is a God who is not squeamish about moral, social and religious taboos. It should come as no surprise, then, to find God speaking or acting through the wise sayings of non-Israelite rulers, for example (Prov. 30), through an ass! (Num. 22.28) or through the political movements of a pagan king. The prophet Isaiah, talking of the pagan ruler Cyrus of Persia, tells us that the Lord 'grasps his right hand', 'opens doors before him' and calls him by name (Isa. 45.1). When archaeologists unearthed the famous Cyrus Cylinder on which Cyrus' conquests were recorded they found him giving thanks and praise to the Babylonian god Marduk for giving him Babylon! Yet Isaiah even has the effrontery to call this same Cyrus the Lord's 'anointed' or 'messiah'! The point then is that, uncomfortable as it may be for us, we cannot predetermine who is and who is not a suitable candidate to mediate God's presence. The Holy Spirit who is the presence of God in the world is like the wind that 'blows where it wills' (John 3.8).

Part of the discomfort we may feel with the above is that we need certainty in life. We need some way of telling what is and what is not God's will for us. I am presently working with a deeply religious person who is thrown into turmoil because he cannot determine which of his thoughts and ideas are from God and which are not. Although his turmoil has deeply psychological roots, it should not be dismissed as entirely neurotic. What criteria do we use to distinguish truth from error? The Wisdom writings are concerned with this question. They too are underpinned by the doctrine of creation declaring 'The Lord by wisdom founded the earth' (Prov. 3.19). Wisdom is the very foundation of creation. The theologian Charles Scobie calls her the 'mediatrix of creation'.[3] That is just where wisdom is found: in creation itself, in the instinctual behaviour of animals (Job 39.13ff.), in the hustle and bustle of human life (Prov. 8.1–3). Here, personified as a prostitute, Wisdom, known to the Greeks as Sophia, calls out to us from the market-place. What imagery! We do not find here a sanitized, morally sensitive God, that we so often hear preached: 'On the heights along the way, where the paths meet, she takes her stand; beside the gates leading into the city, at the entrances, she cries aloud' (Prov. 8.2–3). But 'Folly', similarly, is personified as a 'loose woman'. She too seductively calls out to us from the world: 'She sits at the door of her house, on a seat at the highest point in the city, calling to those who pass by, who go straight on their way' (Prov. 9.14–15).

How then may we be wise? How may we distinguish Folly from Wisdom? They both have a similar appearance. The book of Proverbs goes into great detail on the differences between Wisdom and Folly. 'Happy is the man who finds wisdom . . . she is more precious than jewels . . . her ways are of pleasantness, and all her paths are peace. She is a tree of life to those who lay hold of her . . . keep sound wisdom and discretion . . . they will be life for your soul.' Again: (s)he 'who finds me finds life'. Folly, on the other hand, although she has lips that 'drip honey . . . in the end she is as bitter as wormwood . . . Her feet go down to death . . . she does not take heed of the path of life; her ways wander and she does not know it' (Prov. 3.13–22; 8.35; 5.3–6).

The two metaphors of Life and Death are employed throughout the first chapters of the book of Proverbs with reference to both Wisdom and Folly. Put simply, Wisdom leads to Life – is an affirmation of Life; Folly, on the other hand, leads to Death. These two metaphors of Life and Death must, I think, be taken holistically. They do not just refer to biological life and death. Life has to do with opening ourselves up to the healing power of God in every dimension: to justice, hope, and liberation from oppression. Death, by contrast, is about closing down life to God. It is the way of enslavement, injustice, tyranny and inhumanity. This, then, is the first thing to say about Wisdom – Wisdom brings life.

Wisdom does not equal scientific knowledge. Scientific knowledge is a 'knowing how' and knowing how is not synonymous with Wisdom. The reduction of Wisdom to scientific knowledge has created a large menacing shadow, as we shall see in a later chapter. It has also led to much Folly, and Folly leads to Death. I can know how to split the atom, but to build up an arsenal of nuclear weapons is surely Folly. I can know how to make aerosols and refrigerators, but to blast holes in the ozone layer is Folly. I can know how to work obsessively to earn much money, but the resulting damage to my soul is Folly. Wisdom may have a strong element of 'know how' about it but it is also much more – more mysterious, more intuitive, more involving of feelings, more instinctual (see, for example, Job 39.13ff.) – 'I see feelingly' said the blind Earl of Gloucester to King Lear. Wisdom cannot be reduced to a set of 'know how' rules or instructions any more than we can make a Stradivarius violin by following plans or ride a bicycle by reading instructions.

Biblical Wisdom, as Sophia, is depicted as feminine playfulness. We are told to 'embrace her'. Then she 'will place on your head a fair garland' (Prov. 4.8–9). Play lies at the foundation of creation. At the beginning, when God was giving order to the world, Sophia was there 'playing as a young child' (Prov. 8.30). We should be careful here. Because Sophia is to do with feminine playfulness this should not (mis)lead us. Jung believed the feminine and masculine are two psychological principles that belong to both men and women. He called the masculine principle 'animus' and the feminine principle 'anima', after the Latin. The immediate important implication is that 'feminine' does not equate with 'female' or 'woman'. Both men and women need to engage with playful Sophia in themselves. The loss of playfulness is a tragic consequence of our patriarchal and dryly rationalistic modern world, as we shall see later. I am reminded of a story: a mother and her young children were attending a particularly long-drawn-out and boring church service. The children had been restless for some time. They begged their mother to let them go outside and play. In the end she yielded. Ten minutes later God went out to join them!

The title of this book aims to capture the playful aspect of Wisdom. It is not meant to imply triviality. The subject of the shadow includes some of the most deeply painful and horrific aspects of human life. Even so, playful Sophia may be present. When Jesus – the crucified one – is portrayed as a clown or 'Lord of the Dance', we are alerted to the fact that Sophia is present in the depths of human suffering. 'Despair Doesn't Dance . . .' was the title of an article that caught my eye. But I think that you can dance despair. It is a very special kind of dance. After several months in counselling, a woman of great courage knew the time had come for her to engage with her despair over the loss of her father whom she admired and loved greatly. She went home, drew the curtains, made a simple altar with candles and a crucifix. She took out from her cupboard a scarf that her father had once bought her. She put on the scarf and before the altar danced her despair – a mournful sorrowful dance which released a healing flood of tears of grief.

Wisdom bids us 'walk in the way of insight' (Prov. 9.6). She is about education. *Educo* in Latin means 'I lead out'. Contrast *educo* with *seduco*, which means 'I lead aside'. Here is the difference between Wisdom and Folly. Wisdom is educative, Folly leads us astray. Wisdom 'has sent out her maids to call from the highest places in the town'; she says, 'Come, eat of my bread and drink of the wine I have mixed . . . and walk in the way of insight' (Prov. 9.3–6). The one who accepts Wisdom's invitation is truly the philosopher, for this is the meaning of the word (literally 'lover of Sophia'). The one who goes after Folly is the simpleton and the fool (Prov. 2.22; 9.16). Folly, after appeasing her conscience with religious observances, says, 'I have come out to meet you, to seek you eagerly . . . With much seductive speech she persuades him . . . he does not know that it will cost him his life' (Prov. 7.15–23).

When we say Wisdom is about education we do not mean a dry, rationalistic, sitting-in-rows, learning-facts type of education. We mean a playful, dancing education. When we experience the thrill, the tingle down the spine of the 'aha', or even the 'ha-ha' experience that comes with insight, Sophia has danced with us. I recall a time when I turned the television on halfway through a scientific documentary. The documentary showed that by using a computer program based on the theory of evolution, we eventually arrive at the perfect shape for a propeller. I was completely enthralled. The beautifully constructed gleaming propeller was literally awesome and I felt what can only be called a deeply religious sensation. Struck by the wonder of creation, I was moved to worship God. At this point the commentator announced that the computer had validated the theory of evolution and that this proved once and for all that there is no God! I was speechless. I had been unwittingly watching atheistic propaganda! How dry and serious was the presenter! How he had sucked sacred play out of his secular science. What irony! I fell about laughing. Sophia with a teasing glint in her eye had whirled me round in a reel.

The New Testament gives us some further clues on how to recognize Wisdom. 'Wisdom from above is first pure, then peaceable, gentle, open to reason, full of mercy and good fruits, without uncertainty or insincerity' (Jas. 3.17).

Wisdom is 'peaceable and gentle'. In working with the shadow these two aspects of Wisdom are especially important. So often we want to whip ourselves over the way we find ourselves behaving. Many times I have said to someone as they have left a counselling session 'Do not be too hard on yourself.' The temptation to reject our shadow is overwhelmingly strong. To dance with the shadow requires Wisdom.

Wisdom is 'open to reason' and 'without uncertainty'. We may note an important paradox in these words. We are to be both certain and open to reason at the same time: certain that God will give us Wisdom and open to reason as we seek to discover what that Wisdom is. Any hard-headed, dogmatic dismissing of ideas or theories about life is a consorting with Folly, not Wisdom. The Wisdom from above is more aware of what it does not know. Wisdom chastens us when we claim privileged access to the divine will. Wisdom knows that it 'sees through a glass darkly'. Wisdom says 'I take myself seriously, but not too seriously.' The writer John Caputo notes: 'The one mistake that Socrates found among the politicians, craftsmen, and artists [of ancient Greece] was that they took themselves and their opinions seriously – always a deadly flaw, putting an end to the play, an end to the discussion.'⁴ Being a counsellor or therapist is tutelage in Wisdom as humility. We soon learn to lay aside quick and clever theories and insights into a person's behaviour. We learn to wait in humility before the soul.

Wisdom is 'full of mercy and good fruits'. Folly shows neither mercy nor good fruits. Christ, who is called the Wisdom of God in the New Testament, is our example here (1 Cor. 1.24). He went about healing the sick, restoring sight to the blind, making the lame walk and the deaf hear, cleansing lepers, raising the dead and giving the poor good news (Luke 7.22). We know that we are in the presence of Wisdom when we see healing, and the compassion that motivates this is Life.

Finally, but most importantly, Wisdom begins with 'the fear of the Lord' (Prov. 9.10; see also Job 28.28): that is trusting commitment to and reverence for the God of the Scriptures. 'Fear' also points to the holiness of God. Holiness is not primarily a moral concept. God, as Martin Luther said, is beyond good and evil. Holiness is a religious concept. Before a holy God, fear and awe are appropriate emotions. This becomes particularly important when it comes to idolatry. When we trust and revere the Lord we shun idolatry. In a later chapter we will explore the nature of idolatry further. Fear, as we might suppose, does not preclude dance, for the God we are to fear is a God who through Sophia invites us to dance.

Now that we have explored Wisdom a little, let us turn our attention again to Jung. It will be clear from the above that I believe it would be quite wrong to dismiss the work of Jung out of hand on the grounds that he is not an orthodox Christian or that he too has a shadow side. To do so would be to be guilty of what is known in philosophy as the 'generic fallacy' – dismissing a theory because of its origins. Conversely, it would be out of place to try to defend the character of Jung against his critics, although I am tempted. The Bible, as we have seen, takes a different approach. Anything, anyone, and everyone, regardless of their religious beliefs, is a potential mediator of divine disclosure. In the last analysis, like the sheep who know their shepherd (John 10), we know the voice of God because it affirms Life. God called the pagan worshipper Cyrus of Persia his 'anointed' (messiah) because Cyrus allowed exiles to return home and to re-establish their own religions. Cyrus thus reversed the oppressive, life-denying political policy of previous conquerors whose custom was to break the will of their captives by deporting them to other counries. God spoke through the ass of the pagan diviner Balaam to show how his life-giving power and presence are not parochially confined. Similarly, the wise sayings of non-Israelites inserted into the book of Proverbs demonstrate that Wisdom is to be found outside narrowly defined religious confines. I remember my Christian philosophy professor telling his students a parable. The scene is the judgement seat of God. God speaks: 'You have given water to the thirsty and I am well pleased. But, I have this against you: you did not listen to my servant Karl Marx!' We might change this to: 'You did not listen to my servant Carl Jung!'

Only if it can be shown that Jung's theory of the psyche itself leads to Death rather than Life should we hold it at arm's length. The question we must ask then is this: do the ideas of Jung open up Life or do they close down Life?

It is my experience that Jung's ideas of the shadow and working with the shadow do bring Life and healing. Over the years I have worked with many people in counselling. I have found that certain aspects of Jung's theory of the psyche have brought Life to people by helping them come through extremely distressing and confusing circumstances, and indeed I have found this true for myself. It has often been a humbling experience to witness people courageously and painfully engage with their shadows. I have also seen them deepen in compassion in their spirituality and in their sense of God. There are other aspects of Jung's thought which, from a Christian perspective, warrant more careful critical appraisal – a task with which I am also presently engaged but is not the focus of this book. This book turns on what I consider to be the positive aspect of Jung's work: his Wisdom.

I hope also that the above discussion will reveal that not only do I invite the reader to dance with the shadow but also to dance with Sophia. In the second half of this book we will be looking at dreams, fairy tales, active imagination, painting and other ways of dancing with the shadow. To do our shadow work effectively we will need Sophia, her intuitive insight and playfulness; we will need to be open to reason, full of mercy and good fruits; above all we will need to fear the Lord. Before we can learn to dance with the shadow, however, we must explore in depth what we mean by the shadow and how the shadow is formed. To this task we now turn.

3 *Me and My Shadow*

The personal shadow, we will remember, is made up of those parts of ourselves that we disapprove of or are threatened by and are unable to incorporate into our conscious life. In this chapter we will explore the ways personal shadows are made. By personal shadows I mean the shadows that are produced by our own individual life histories. First, we will look at shadow-making in the earliest years of our emotional development. Then we will discuss the way that societies' taboos lead us to force aspects of our experience into the shadows. Finally, we will explore the unique contribution that Jung has made to our understanding of shadow-making.

Let us return to Martin. Martin, we will remember, was caught in an unbearable tension between 'the good boy' and 'the bad boy'. Sometimes the good boy would win the day, then the bad boy would become Martin's shadow. After a while the bad boy would rebel and whisk Martin away into the world of clubs, drugs and late-night raves, and the good boy would become the shadow. The good boy would get moralistic and condemnatory and drive Martin once more into the fold of the 'godly'. How did this pattern of behaviour begin? We begin with the ideas of the psychologist Alice Miller.

In her book *The Drama of Being a Child*, Alice Miller describes the psychological relationship that can occur between a mother and a child. Mothers – like all of us living in an imperfect or, in theological language, 'fallen' world – bring unresolved emotional conflicts into their relationships. The mother, in order to have emotional equilibrium, unconsciously requires her child to behave in a particular way. Certain kinds of behaviour she greets with an adoring smile; other kinds with disapproving coldness.

At the early stage of a child's life, mother is a god-like creature who holds the keys to life and death for the totally dependant infant. To the child the smile is life, the frown is death. So as not to upset mother and to support her in her own insecurities the child learns to reveal only what is approved of: 'I must always be good and measure up to the norm, then there is no risk.'[1] Thus he splits off the 'good child' who gets the smile of Life from 'bad child' who gets the frown of Death.

Here then, we very likely have the origins of Martin's struggles. The smile and frown of mother have become a dynamic of his inner emotional life and with it the tension between 'good boy' and 'bad boy'. Once an emotional dynamic has been set up, it continues to work after we have left both home and our flesh-and-blood mother behind. It continues to play itself out on surrogate mothers – on friends, on spouses and partners and, especially, on God; for God, who is omnipotent, reminds the psyche of the once omnipotent mother. Now, the frown and smile of mother is replaced by the smile and frown of God. Now, it is God who holds the keys of Life and Death and has the ability to cripple us with guilt when we 'misbehave'. Those who are involved in pastoral care know how tightly this kind of dynamic can grip a person. No matter how many Bible verses we read about how 'nothing can separate us from the love of God' or how many of Jesus' parables we hear which demonstrate the unconditional love of God, we just cannot seem to get out of this grip. This is because the problem is not theological, but psychological. Indeed, we can believe one thing but feel quite another. We may believe and confess in church every Sunday that God loves us unconditionally, but we feel as though he watches our every move, meeting all our actions with approval or disapproval. Thus, like Martin, we continue to play out the bad child/good child dynamic into adult life until 'bad child', frustrated at having been cast into the shadows for twenty years, can stand it no more and bursts out into the open for all to see.

Let us now take Alice Miller's insight into shadow-making further into developmental psychology. Psychologists have found that the first six years of life are particularly crucial in emotional development. During these six years they have detected distinct stages of emotional development. Each of these stages presents a unique challenge to the parent–child relationship. We may call the stages respectively: the newborn stage (up to about three months), early infancy (three months to one year), toddlerhood (one to three years), and childhood (three to six years).

In the last chapter I said that God calls us to Life. This is certainly true for the early stages of emotional development. God's call for the newborn child is: 'Let the child be at home, receive Life, feel wanted and loved.' At the very worst the child receives the message: 'You are not wanted or loved.' Some of us hear only this worst message, most of us hear a confusion of both messages. Even the most loving, devoted and caring mother often has to deal with her own powerful, negative emotions as her sometimes demanding child seems like an invading 'monster' to her. The baby picks up the messages which are transmitted through the 'coldness' of the mother's body. If the more powerful message is negative, the child learns that his or her presence is not good. He learns to hide himself – maybe his very bodily presence; certainly those emotions that make his presence noticed, for then he will experience the 'frown' of his mother. As he grows older he will learn ways of defending himself against the pain of rejection. Maybe he will try to 'escape' from his body 'into the head' and into abstract thought – he may pursue the academic life. (Although, of course, not everyone who becomes an academic does so because of early emotional traumas.) He will very likely have a very poor bodily self-image and may experience great difficulties in his personal relationships with others, for his deepest experience of personal relationships is of not being wanted. The rejected feelings, the rejected bodily presence and the rejected need for intimacy build up to form a shadow which may return with a vengeance in later life. Ashley Montague in his classic book *Touching* tells of a woman who turned to prostitution to relieve her unhappiness. She said that she used sex because she wanted to be held.[2] Deprived of loving touch, this woman was driven by an insatiable desire to be wanted.

The early infancy stage is the oral stage. God calls at this stage for the child to be nourished and to know that it is all right to need. Early deprivation may come about by a mother actually dying, or by her emotional withdrawal, because of depression, for example. In such cases the child hears the message: 'Your needs will not be met' or: 'It is bad of you to have needs.' A common defence against the painful feelings of emptiness and abandonment is to deny the feelings and to deny need. Years of denial of the God-given right to need accumulate as shadow. This may burst out in later life in the form of an emotional breakdown when a person is overpowered with feelings of neediness. In adult life, the image of God as 'Mother' who nurtures us, provides for all our needs, and gives us unconditional love, simply for being who we are, is very helpful for meeting those needs.

At the stage of toddlerhood, God calls the child to explore, experiment and to begin to 'stand on his or her own feet'. I have heard this stage described as the call for the child to climb out of the 'maternal swamp'. This sounds too disparaging – 'maternal nest' perhaps is better. However, the nest may turn into a swamp if we fail to respond to the call. In order for the child to go through this stage effectively, the presence of a father-figure is crucial. The father encourages the child to take the step out of maternal symbiosis. I am reminded of the story of Jesus walking on the water, and we remember Jesus' words 'When you have seen me you have seen the Father.' The disciples are in a boat in a storm. They see Jesus walking on the water towards them. Peter wants to go out on the water to meet him. Jesus encourages him. But Peter loses his nerve when he focuses his attention on the storm raging around him and he begins to sink. Jesus reaches out his hand to save him (Matt. 14.22–33).

This process does not necessarily imply the need for a biological father, but a significant person in the child's life, other than the mother, is needed to mediate 'father' to the child. It is a particularly crucial stage for boys, for it involves them in finding their own separate gender identity. Some men, it seems, have never really separated themselves from mother. They remain for ever tangled, turning wives, girlfriends and work colleagues into surrogate mothers. Love affairs for such a man often involve a kind of clinging which is to do with the small child in him that has never left the 'maternal swamp'. The writer Robert Bly, in his best seller *Iron John*, believes that our modern world has made it particularly hard for a boy child to find his masculine identity. Before the Industrial Revolution, Bly argues, the father was more physically present. The time would come when the boy would stand by the side of his father learning the trade – of blacksmith or carpenter. Thus he would learn the 'rhythms of the masculine'. Nowadays, children are lucky if they see their father before six or seven at night. By that time it is bedtime, and besides the father is exhausted from work and commuting.[3]

For a girl child the separation from mother does not involve her in finding her own gender identity, but it does involve her in finding her own psychological identity and independence. Many adult women still find themselves struggling to tear themselves away from mother. A woman I have worked with once produced a painting. She used so much water with her blue paint that the paper was awash until it crinkled up. She said 'This is mother', pointing to the swamp she had painted. I asked her where she was in the painting. She painted one small brown speck in the middle! For a girl, father is still important. Like Jesus in the story of Jairus' daughter, he holds out his hand and encourages her to step out and find her separate identity.

I believe that many of us find this stage in life 'unfinished'. This, I believe, points up the psychological need for male imagery for God. As adults we need to engage with the fatherhood of God – to draw encouragement from the one who says 'Step out, you can do it.' We have, I think, been misled by the popular wisdom that the Aramaic word 'Abba' as used by Jesus and the apostle Paul refers to the inarticulate babbling of an infant. This belief has encouraged a spirituality of immature dependence. The theologian James Barr recently has shown that 'Abba' as a term for father was used in formal, adult contexts.[4] While the word does undoubtedly imply a relationship of close intimacy it does not imply childishness or childish dependence. It would be more helpful psychologically if 'Abba' conveyed the image of the God who lovingly calls us out of an infantile entanglement with mother towards adulthood.

If the call of God at the stage of toddlerhood is to explore, step out and to begin to be one's own person, the conflicting message comes in the form of excessive and heavy-handed reprimands and shaming when explorations and adventures result in mishap. Such traumas may result in an inability to step out and take initiative for fear of shaming. The creative, playful impulse is then stifled and builds up in the shadows. Or, as we have suggested, it may result in a fear to grow up to adulthood.

The childhood stage is the stage of sexual awareness. God's call is for the child to be affirmed in her sexuality. Since people in our modern society are quite sexually confused, he may well hear a conflicting message. The young sexually aware child crawls sensually on to her father's lap. If he is not comfortable with his own sexuality he 'freezes' or tenses his body against her. She senses that she is now not loved freely in the way she used to be. The message she hears is: 'Your sexuality is not good', or rather, and this is important: 'Now that you are a sexual being, *you* are not good.' Our sexuality is not something we have: this is an erroneous way of thinking of our sexuality and our bodiliness. We shall explore this view in more depth in a later chapter. Our sexuality is something we are. A child especially is not able to abstract her sexuality from her identity. The underlying hurt pride may give rise to a tendency to stubborness and also to an inability to love freely from the heart. It may also result in the splitting-off of sex from love and even in promiscuity, for the underlying fear is 'If I am sexual with the one I love then I will be rejected.' Thus sexuality is pushed down into the shadows. Of course, there is also the possibility of the opposite distortion of the sexual call of God at this stage. This occurs when the child is sexually abused. Our modern sexually confused society means that this also happens all too often, as we have all lately become very aware.

Deep traumas then, experienced at different stages in our early emotional development, result in various kinds of shadows. However, personal shadow-making does not stop at the age of six years or so, the process goes on through later life. Schools, for example, can be a factory for shadow-making. I remember, to my shame, standing with a group of lads jeering as a naked boy was pulled and kicked around the shower-room floor. The watching group had become demonic in its spirit, catching us all up in an infectious frightening madness – maybe it was the twisted thrill of watching someone else rather than ourselves being shamed and humiliated. Maybe our own vulnerability had leapt out of the shadows on to him where we could hate and despise it without being humiliated ourselves. The victim was a particularly vulnerable boy, not good at sports or academically bright. God knows what torments he suffered that day and because of it. Very likely in order to survive he had to push his humiliated self and all his feelings of shame and rage into the shadows. Another young man I know was sexually assaulted at knife point when he was a young boy at school. It took months in counselling before he felt able to retrieve this experience from the shadows.

Religious, moral and social taboos also play their part in shadow-making. Staying with the subject of sexuality: a young woman struggles to accept her sexuality and her embarrassment about her body. She grew up in a strict religious family. Sex, as many of us are now aware, has been too readily linked with sinfulness. The subject of sex was never discussed openly in her home except in a negative way. This religious pressure succeeded in pushing her sexuality into the shadows. Another woman now in her thirties regrets a decision she made when she was nineteen – to be celibate. She was convinced then that this was God's will for her – there is a theme in Christian tradition (mistaken) that God prefers (smiles at!) the celibate life. Now she realizes that this theological rationalization hid the real reason for her decision. She had a poor self-image and deep down she believed that no one would want her. This fear, unconscious as it was at the time, had driven her to her decision – unconsciously she would make herself unavailable before anyone had the chance to reject her. In these two examples we may have a very subtle collusion between an early childhood trauma – parents emotionally unable to handle the emerging sexual identity of their daughters – and a religious pressure. In the last case the resulting mix created a powerful shadow of a disowned need for intimacy.

I think the most poignant expression I have heard regarding taboos and shadow-making came from the lips of a gay man. 'Discovering I was gay was like discovering that I was that person my mother had always warned me about!' The pressure of social, moral and religious taboos against gay sexuality is so immense that it can create the most dreadful shadow behaviour. Homophobia can be vicious. John Boswell records in his book *Homosexuality and Intolerance* how in the Middle Ages a succession of disasters, including the failure of the crusades, meant that certain minority groups were persecuted. Homosexuals were one of these persecuted groups.[5] God, it was thought, had deserted the people because of the presence of 'deviant' groups. Looking for someone to blame – otherwise known as scapegoating – is typical shadow activity. The most likely victims are those who are different from the majority. We are reminded at this point of Jesus' concern for the minority groups in the society of his day. He continued a theme found in the Old Testament. There too God is concerned for the minorities – the downtrodden and oppressed. Another gay man, now in his late forties, had engraved into his face the lines of stress wrought by hiding away his true identity. He told of how years earlier, after much torment, he confessed to his doctor that he feared that he was homosexual. The doctor responded by saying, 'I find this completely disgusting. The Greek civilization foundered because of rampant homosexuality!' This poor man did not dare confide in another soul for a further twenty years, but suffered, hiding himself away with the label 'unacceptable to society'.

Another social taboo is 'mental illness'. More than once I have worked with someone who has been 'sectioned' to a mental hospital at one time in his or her life. What a dreadful word 'sectioned' is. Originally it was a legal category and referred to a 'section' of an Act of Parliament, but it lives on as a shadow term meaning 'cut off from the rest'. The stigma that people who have been 'sectioned' carry through life is terrifying. They are always afraid someone will find out. The pressure upon them leads them to believe that they are somehow deeply flawed – marked for ever – always fearful that a bout of depression means that their 'illness' will return and they will be put away again.

One such person came to me saying she was weary of trying to hide her past. The burden, carried for the last twenty-odd years, had finally worn her out – trying to appear sane to everyone so that they will not cut her off again. Another man's shadow of 'mental illness' would burst forth in terrified paranoia when he became convinced that whispers in the corridors at work were about him. In fact these two were among the most deeply sane people I have met. They both had touched the edges of human life in a way many of us never do, giving them a depth of feeling, a courage and compassion that is rare. It is the attitude of the rest of us to these people that has in part forced them to carry their past as a shadowy burden. It seems to me that ex-psychoanalyst Jeffrey Masson has a point when he says:

> I do not subscribe to the position that there are people who are mentally ill and require 'real treatment', meaning psychiatric drugs . . . and then there are the rest of us, who merely need to be talked to. I believe, on the contrary, that while there is no such medical entity as mental illness, there are innumerable kinds of suffering and terrible emotional pain that many people, in fact most, undergo at some time or various times in their lives.[6]

Maybe Masson goes too far; there are people who are more prone to be drawn across the border into psychosis than others and we will discuss this later, but his point is well taken. The phrases 'mental illness' and 'sectioned' probably have more to do with an unconscious fear concerning the maintenance of power of the majority who define sanity, a point to which we will also return. We would all do well to hear these words of Jung: 'The things that come to light brutally in insanity remain hidden in the background in neurosis, but they continue to influence consciousness nonetheless.'[7] And which one of us does not sometimes behave neurotically?

Again, we are all aware of sexual stereotyping. When this occurs, so does shadow-making. Women who are not allowed formal leadership over men have their initiative and power pushed into the shadows, from where it begins to operate manipulatively. A young man I knew wanted to go to art school. His parents were anxious that he should get a well-paid career so he could support his future wife and family. They bullied him into becoming an electronics engineer. After ten agonizing and wasted years (although of course a lot can happen in 'wasted time'), the artist in him could no longer stand the repression and burst out, whisking him off to drama college. Men who 'must not cry' have their sensitive emotional selves forced into the shadows. From the hidden depths it continues to drive them, tossing them first here, then there – or worse. The theologian James Nelson makes his point sharply:

> The emotional damage done to men through the de-
> pravation of feelings is enormous, and it takes its toll in
> violence . . . . As little boys, men are taught that 'big
> boys don't cry,' and that when threatened or hurt they
> should learn to 'stand up and fight like a man.' Being
> deprived of human tears, they, in turn, victimize
> women as a means to live out this impossible cultural
> assignment to control the feminine in themselves.[8]

One of my clients is struggling to admit his repressed feminine side into his personality – to dance with his feminine shadow. He told me of his first years at secondary school. He was a village lad who had passed the eleven-plus. This meant that he had to say goodbye to all his friends and set off to the tough town grammar school on his own. He recounted his first impressions of his new school – how cold and impersonal it was, how harsh and even violent appeared the teachers and town boys. The great challenge was not to let the gathering tears show. He managed and learned to be macho; that is until he joined

the army. The night before his last day of training he had
got drunk with some of the others and was arrested by a
policeman for disturbing the peace. Next day, while he
was standing with the others to attention in the barrack
room, the training sergeant positioned himself inches away
from his face bawling out a tirade of humiliating adjec-
tives. The threshold was crossed and my client broke
down in tears. The disgrace, the ridicule, the stigma – he
had committed the unforgivable sin and for all to see –
he had cried. The news spread quickly and from then on
he was a marked man.

Thus, and in so many ways, shadows are made. Yet it
is not only traumas experienced in earlier years nor is it
just families' and societies' taboos that make personal
shadows. In order to understand shadow-making more
fully we need to explore Jung's theory of the human
psyche. In particular we need to unpack Jung's key concepts of the 'ego', 'the personal unconscious', the 'collective unconscious', and 'archetypes'.[9]

Imagine an iceberg – a small amount is visible above the
water, yet we know that going down into the depths there
is a vast area that we cannot see. The human psyche may
be compared to an iceberg. What is visible is all that we are
conscious of. Jung called the centre of our conscious
awareness, the 'ego'. The ego lies at the interface of the
psyche and the outside world. In popular speaking we
think of the ego in rather negative terms. We tend to link
it with our pride. When we say our ego is hurt we mean
that our pride is hurt. Hurt pride is about ego inflation. In
Jung's more precise use of the term the ego is, rather, an
essential part of the human psyche. The ego is that part of
us that feels and thinks and imagines and plans and
speaks. It is that part of ourselves which says 'I'. Many
people today think that our ego is all there is to us. To use
a computer metaphor, we live in a WYSIWYG ('What you
see is what you get') world. Jung disagrees. He came to

believe that the vast amount of our psyche is unconscious. It lies below the surface. We cannot see it at all. First, there is the 'personal unconscious'. In the personal unconscious lie all the painful feelings from our early individual emotional experience that we outlined above and that have been pushed out of our conscious awareness. However, as we have already discussed, these suppressed traumatic feelings continue to drive us right into adult life.

Beneath the personal unconscious lies the 'collective unconscious'. The hypothesis of the collective unconscious is Jung's unique contribution to psychology. According to Jung, the collective unconscious makes up the greater part of the psyche. The term 'collective' points to the fact that this part of the human psyche is common to all of us. Jung advanced his theory of the collective unconscious after studying carefully and thoroughly the legends, mythologies and fairy tales of different cultures. He found that these revealed common themes. For example, the hero theme can be traced through many cultures – Odysseus, Siegfried, Mabinogion, Sir Galahad, Percival and the Holy Grail, George and the dragon, etc. Jung also discovered that these same themes consistently appeared in the dreams of his patients.

According to Jung, then, the human psyche has a common foundational structure. This means that in large part our psychological experience will conform to recognizable patterns. This is not such an exotic theory as has often been made out. In other dimensions of human life we take a common structure for granted. Consider our bodily make-up, for example: we all have arms, legs, organs of a certain size, etc. Indeed, if some of these are lacking or diverge from the pattern we speak of disability. Jung is drawing our attention to the fact that our emotional life too has a structure. This brings us on to the related concept of 'archetype'.

Jung applied the name 'archetypes' to the common patterns that structure our emotional experience. The first thing to note about archetypes is that they are pure forms of experience – that is, they lack content. The content is supplied through *images* from our own individual experience and of a particular place and culture. Put another way, archetypes are clothed in different ways for different people at different times and in different places. However, undress the images and we find the same archetypes. The 'clothes' in which the archetypes appear in human experience, in myths, fairy tales and legends, are to be understood as 'archetypal images'. We may speak of 'the warrior', 'the king' and, as already mentioned, 'the hero' archetypal image. Not all heroes and their adventures appear the same, but the image is formed by the same archetype. Nor are all hero dream images identical but the archetypal patterning ensures a continuity between them.

Before we go on to discuss archetypes further let us catch our breath and try to recap on Jung's theory of the psyche. A diagram may help to clarify this:

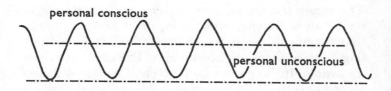

personal conscious

personal unconscious

archetypes of the
collective unconscious

Jung's Theory of the Psyche

The two broken lines represent the fact that the divisions between the three aspects of the psyche – conscious awareness with the ego at the centre, the personal unconscious with all the suppressed painful feelings from our earlier personal histories, and the collective unconscious with the archetypes – are 'porous'. There may be movement between them. The fact that the membranes dividing the three aspects of the psyche are not impervious is crucial for understanding both shadow-making and how we may 'dance with the shadow'. It means, first, that we can push down the most painful emotional experiences from our own individual histories through the membrane and into the personal unconscious. These then form the personal shadow, as we have seen. Second, it means that these suppressed emotions are able to leak through and continue to affect our lives. They may even sometimes flood through. Then the ego bobs about like a cork on the tide of released emotions. Third, the fact that the membranes are porous means that the archetypes of the collective unconscious have access to the personal unconscious and to the ego, and through the ego to the outside world. This means that we – our ego selves – can become caught up by an archetype. Archetypes, or archetypal images, have 'numinous' power – they have a fascinating, compelling, even spiritual aura about them. This can make them irresistible. In Jung's words: 'The chief danger is that of succumbing to the fascinating influence of the archetypes.'[10] In a later chapter we will see how this important aspect of the nature of archetypes can help us to understand in a deeper way the meaning of the cross of Christ.

One of the clearest examples of the numinous power of archetypes is that of falling in love. Those of us who have fallen in love, and it can happen to anyone, will know what it is to be in the grip of an archetype. No matter what we do we seem unable to disentangle ourselves. It is as though we give our very soul away to the one we love.

Sometimes this is so compelling that we end up by sacrificing everything – our moral and religious values, our friends, our respectability, our careers. Stories abound of people who have fallen in love with someone who is 'out of bounds'. Their feelings are so intense that they have turned their world upside down for the one they love.

When we are in love we find ourselves doing things that otherwise we would deride or feel ashamed of: we go miles out of our way just for a glimpse of our beloved; the superficial poetry and sentimental lyrics of pop songs take on new deep heartfelt meaning – it is as though now we suddenly understand! We catch a scent of the perfume that our lover also wears and our hearts reel. 'O, so light afoot Will ne'er wear out the everlasting Flint. A lover may bestride the gossamer That idles in the wanton summer air, And yet not fall; so light is vanity.' Thus says Shakespeare's Friar Lawrence about Romeo and Juliet. Things seem to get out of all proportion. Our friends whisper 'What on earth does she see in him?' 'People who are not in love fail to understand how an intelligent man can suffer because of a very ordinary woman,' writes Marcel Proust. To the one who is in love the 'very ordinary woman' is like a goddess. She has an irresistible erotic fascination, a deep wisdom and an immortality that belongs only to the gods – this love, we think, will last for ever. Archetypes can be seen, in a way, as gods of the psyche. Jung believed that the gods of Greek mythology and of other ancient cultures were in fact psychological realities projected on to the world outside. When we examine the behaviour of the gods, we learn much about the dynamics of the human psyche. The psyche, then, is where Olympus, the home of the gods, is to be found and when Aphrodite – the goddess of love – appears, who can resist her divine power? Many times she has wreaked havoc, leaving a trail of broken marriages and broken hearts.

One part of us sees the craziness of love, or rather infatuation, and with great moral resolve we decide to resist love's pulls: we will break all contact with our beloved. Then the other part of ourselves puts pressure on us until we can stand the separation from our beloved no more. Then children, husbands, wives, home, career, church and friends are sacrificed in a moment and we run away with our beloved. More than once I have sat with someone in counselling – men and women – as through tears and wringing of hands they have cried out their misery. They are caught in limbo, an unbearable tension. If they burn their bridges and run off with their beloved they will for ever feel guilty; although some do so run off. If they cut all ties with their beloved they will dwell for ever in regret of true love lost; or that is how it seems. Brutal cutting off like this can result in dreadful humiliation as we burst into floods of uncontrollable grief in front of everyone. Maya Angelou describes this experience vividly in her poem 'Prescience':

> Had I known the heart would leak,
> Slobbering its sap, with vulgar
> Visibility, into the dressed-up
> Dining rooms of strangers . . .[11]

Sometimes we oscillate backwards and forwards, maybe for years; leaving home for a while, returning home again, then going off again as we are buffeted around first by grief, then by guilt, then by grief again.

The counselling task is to 'hold' a person who is caught in the grip of love against archetypal buffeting. We hold both sides of them, as Jesus did the children. We do not side with one part of them or the other. That would be a mistake, for, as in Martin's case, our unconscious often moves us to seek counselling from whoever will support us in our current orientation. When that orientation switches, then we go to someone else. The counsellor needs to stay as neutral, or, better, as non-judgemental as possible. The time will come when the ego is able to gain a foothold in the swirling torrent of feeling. When that happens it is as if we begin to come out from under a spell. The scales fall from our eyes. We see that our idols have clay feet. The god or goddess becomes merely mortal. In the language of Jungian psychology, we begin to see that we were possessed by a god of the psyche, by Aphrodite. She somehow became fused with the real person. In psychological terms we projected Aphrodite on to the other.

> Thou hast transferred
> To her dull form awhile
> My beauty, fame, and deed, and word,
> My gestures and my smile.

Thus says the sprite of Thomas Hardy's rather pessimistic poem 'The Well-Beloved' about his bride to be. We will discuss more fully the important topic of projection later on.

I am not suggesting that we should never have anything to do with Aphrodite or that 'falling in love' is a bad thing. A life which is never touched by Aphrodite would be a dull life indeed. As we shall see later, the trick is to dance with the gods of the psyche, not to let them whisk us off the dance floor.

I believe that in order for us to escape the powerful grip of archetypes a deep sense of the reality of God is crucial. A genuine belief in God will enable us to see that Aphrodite is not omnipotent; life will not come to an end if we are not for ever with our beloved. Nor, it must be said, will all life end if we do make such a choice. We need to see that two archetypes are at work here. One we have named Aphrodite. She tells us that Life is to be found only through our lover. The other is the archetype of the critical parent. This archetype tells us that the way of Aphrodite leads to certain 'death'. He says that Life is to be found only when we completely renounce the side of ourselves that is so intoxicated with love. We must, he insists, conform to the strict moral law – no ifs or buts. If we do not, 'Just think,' he says, 'what everyone will think of us.' Our ego sides with one archetype and then the other, tossed to and fro like Martin was. God, however, sides with neither. Our ego finds true Life only in God, not by succumbing to the seduction of any archetype. Thus God helps to free us from the grip of both archetypes. Only then can a genuine, morally responsible, decision be made.

Before we can reach such a decision, however, we may have to do some deep searching into our own personal emotional history to see why we are so ruthlessly caught up in a war of the gods of the psyche. Possession by archetypes may catch us by surprise, but the shadows in our own personal unconscious are most likely the first cause of this, as the following story of Geoffrey and Lynn illustrates. The story also illustrates the fascinating power of archetypes. Geoffrey was a competent and successful businessman in his mid-fifties. He was also a churchwarden. He had been married for more than twenty years and had grown-up children and grandchildren. He came for counselling because he was at a complete loss to explain what was happening to him. Christmas had come and, like so many years before, it was time for the office party. As is his custom, he had bought little gifts for the 'girls' in the office, giving them a kiss on the cheek as he handed them over. Sue had worked there for many years. Geoffrey gave her the present with the customary kiss on the cheek. Before either of them knew what was happening, they were locked in a passionate embrace. Three weeks later, and to the astonishment and disdain of all those around him, Geoffrey left his wife and home. Sue also left her husband and they set up house together.

Geoffrey and Sue spent three months together. Then one day Geoffrey rang home to sort out an administrative problem and heard the voice of his grandchild in the background. Within two days he was back home. In archetypal language, Aphrodite was chased off by Hera, the goddess of the family. Hera, in mythology, spent much of her time persecuting her husband's mistresses. Sue also returned to her husband. At this point Geoffrey came for counselling, bewildered – archetypes can lead us a sorry dance, flitting in, whirling us around in their numinous power, and then taking their leave. Almost his first words were: 'I have always been in control of my life. I have managed people and my business with confidence and authority yet I do not know what is happening to me – I have completely lost control.' Geoffrey had met the formidable power of archetypes. He was being played with by the 'gods' of the psyche.

Geoffrey's wife Lynn had been brought up in a strict religious family. Sex was never openly talked about and she had always had an ambivalent attitude towards her own sexuality. She confessed that sex scared her. Geoffrey said that he was initially attracted to Lynn because he thought she was 'pure and moral'. Sex had never been a significant part of their relationship and both of them said that it was not that important to them.

After many years of painful work in counselling, Geoffrey and Lynn decided to split up. Geoffrey later met someone else and settled down. Lynn went away to Malaysia for a year and fell passionately in love. When she came back she said she was a 'different woman'. She felt as if she were a teenager again. She said that now she could hardly contain her sexual impulse.

By failing to engage with and even suppressing a God-given aspect of their human nature – their sexuality – the lives of both Lynn and Geoffrey had cast a long shadow down through the years. Geoffrey often referred to the time when Sue whispered in his ear that she wanted to seduce him. He said that at that moment it was as though floodgates had sprung open and feelings of deep joy long forgotten bubbled to the surface: 'It was too good to be true, that a woman would ever want me in that way.' In archetypal imagery – Aphrodite had sought her revenge after years of suppression. In mythology she is notorious for hounding those who scorn love. In the opening scene of Euripides' *Hippolytus*, Aphrodite announces: 'I stir up trouble for any who ignore me, or belittle me, and who do it out of stubborn pride.' Indeed, hell knows no fury like a woman scorned! It took a trip away for a year for Lynn to discover and engage with her shadow. She found it in Malaysia. This is not so strange. Sir Laurens van der Post tells how a trip away to a non-European country can sometimes put a person in touch with the unlived parts of themselves. In places such as Malaysia and Africa people are much more in touch with what is largely unconscious for us in the West – a deep sensuality and earthy spirituality. Jung himself went to Africa and found a part of himself that he had never imagined existed.[12]

I have focused on the subject of love to illustrate the power of archetypes. Space permitting we could point to countless other examples. Whenever we feel in the grip of some mood that we cannot seem to get out of an archetype is present. I recall a young man who came for counselling. I can only describe him as being in the grip of 'the cynic' archetype. He was thoroughly cynical about almost everything: his church, his friends, religion. Although he came freely to counselling, the cynic had lodged itself at the centre of his psyche from the beginning. Everything that took place in the counselling room he dismissed with a shrug of the shoulders. The cynic so pervaded the room that sometimes I also began to feel cynical. I got the impression that this was a powerful defence against some deep pain, but the archetypal grip was too formidable to penetrate. In the next chapter we will look at another archetype that has held a whole culture in its grip for hundreds of years.

Jung's theories of the collective unconscious and archetypes, then, deepen our understanding of shadow-making. When we suppress or do not engage with archetypes they, like the shadow in Jung's dream, take on gigantic proportions. The time then comes when they may 'leap out', disrupting our well-ordered and respectable lives, catching us in an iron grip, and causing us to behave and feel in ways that we do not want. Before we move on to consider the collective shadow, we should consider the extreme case of archetypal possession – psychosis.

Jung's caution against getting caught up by the fascination of archetypes is brought well home in psychosis. This is when the ego, as it were, gets 'sucked through' the membrane that divides us from the collective unconscious, to be possessed by the gods of the psyche. Many people have psychotic episodes in life. They fall through the membrane to remain in the realm of the collective unconscious until such a time as the ego has enough strength to disentangle itself. Others, sadly, fall through and remain in permanent psychosis. Psychotic episodes are characterized by such attitudes as paranoia – 'everyone is out to get me', or alternatively grandiosity – 'I am the greatest'. A person suffering from psychosis is not aware that they are acting from 'below the membrane'. Once a young man came to see me and said that he was mentally ill. He was convinced that he was a manic-depressive. I felt that his self-diagnosis was wrong. This was confirmed a little later when he came in and told me that he was going through a manic stage. A mentally ill person, if we can use that phrase, does not speak in such a way. Their ego is so identified with the manic archetype that they believe they are sane and normal. They are unable to take distance to reflect as this young man did.

When we are in the presence of a person suffering from psychosis we also meet the formidable power of archetypes. How easy it is for us to be played with by the gods of the psyche too. The seduction can be very subtle. It may begin with a phone call. A person in distress calls upon us to help. We may offer a bed for the night or a meal. We listen sympathetically to a tale involving one misfortune after another. Usually the tale will include instances of bad treatment at the hands of others. We are assured that we are not like the others; we are caring and compassionate. It all sounds so reasonable. Later we find that the first phone call opened the floodgates. Our help is sought more and more. Soon we find we are caught in a trap. We begin to feel totally responsible for the life of this poor soul. It feels like a bottomless pit. We can never do enough: we answer phone calls in the middle of the night, we go out in the pouring rain to sort out an argument. Then we put on the answering machine. We begin to lie – 'Tell him I am not in.' We start to feel guilty. Psychotic people have an almost uncanny way of knowing when we are trying to keep out of their way. They let us know that they know and our guilt increases. A violent person may begin to threaten us. Pretty soon we find that we are just like the others who did not come through for them.

'Borderline' is the term used for those who experience psychosis; they hover around the border, or in our terminology 'membrane', between sanity and insanity.[13] Working with borderline people calls for much wisdom, skill and firm boundaries, and is most often best left to the professional counsellor.

I have discussed the subject of 'borderline' or psychosis not only because it makes us aware of the power of archetypes but also for two other reasons. First, the recent government policy of 'Care in the Community' means that some of us will belong to a community that has borderline people within it, without having any guidelines about how best to relate to them. The other reason is that if we ourselves are going through a period in which we are experiencing psychotic episodes, we should exercise great caution in following the suggestions made in the second half of this book in particular. It would be better for us to seek help and guidance from a professional counsellor or therapist at this point in our lives.

Finally on the subject of the borderline, I do not mean to imply by the above that we should wash our hands of borderline people. A friend of mine who works as a psychotherapist recently went to a workshop on the subject of therapy. One of the leaders made the comment that therapists should stay away from borderline people. The woman sitting next to him began to weep. Her daughter had been diagnosed as borderline. While we may understand the worry that lies behind such a statement, I cannot believe that the only option for psychotic people is a psychiatric ward. Surely this must be only a last resort. Christ opened his arms to all, so should not also the Christian counsellor?

I have touched a number of times on the relationship between the ego and the unconscious. This relationship is crucial and the second half of this book focuses just on this. First, however, we will examine what happens when a whole culture gets caught in the grip of an archetype. To this we now turn.

4 *In the Shadow of Apollo*

In the last chapter we explored the ways in which shadows are made in our individual lives. In this chapter we explore the collective shadow of Western technological society. To do this effectively we need to take both a theological and a psychological perspective. At the outset I want to stress that these two perspectives are not opposed to each other, nor is the one 'spiritual' and the other 'secular'. We stand before God on holy ground when we do psychology just as much as when we do theology. Taking these two perspectives not only will help us understand shadow-making more fully; it will also help us understand the crucial role of Christ in shadow work. First, taking a theological perspective, we need to examine the link between idolatry and shadow-making.[1]

Idolatry, according to the first great Christian theologian, the apostle Paul, is the worshipping and serving of created things rather than the Creator. (Rom. 1.25) When we give ultimate allegiance to something, when we make it the most important thing in our lives, when we trust it to give our lives meaning and purpose, we are worshipping that thing. Paul assumed there were only two options for humanity. Either we worship the Creator or we worship a creature. There is no sitting on the fence. Human beings are worshipping beings. That is how we are created.

In the days of the apostle Paul, idolatry was associated with graven images. Thus Paul says 'Claiming to be wise, they became fools, and exchanged the glory of the immortal God for images resembling mortal man or birds or animals or reptiles' (Rom. 1.22–5). Today, gods are more secular but nevertheless gods they are. The psychologist of religion James Fowler lists some candidates for idolatrous worship: 'Work, prestige and recognition, power and influence, wealth ... family, university, nation, or church. Love, sex and a loved partner . . . .'[2] Any one of these may become our god, that thing which gives our life ultimate meaning and purpose. I remember listening to the chairman of one of the great motor companies. He was being interviewed on the radio. The interviewer asked him how he could justify taking such a massive salary. I was struck by the chairman's answer: 'The market decides what a job is worth.' Here we find evidence of idolatrous worship – of the market. Notice how the market is personified; it speaks. Notice how we are to bow down to it. The god we worship determines our values for us. We the worshippers simply obey.

It is ironic perhaps that the goodness of creation, it seems, provides the occasion for idolatry. 'And God saw everything that he had made, and behold, it was very good' (Gen. 1.31). So the Genesis story of creation reaches its climax. Here we are being asked to take note, or marvel at, how good creation is. In Psalm 8, the Psalmist reflects upon the wonders of creation with human nature its crowning glory. In Psalm 139 the Psalmist declares 'Wonderful are thy works'. In Psalm 148, creation itself is bidden to praise its Maker. Whenever we discover a wonder of creation, if we are not careful we can become dazzled by the light we have found. Our new discovery is all that we see. Wonder and insight tempt us to think that our discovery is the key that unlocks the ultimate mysteries of the universe.

To return to the story of the television documentary on the construction of the perfect propeller of a couple of chapters ago: the wonder and power of computer technology together with the idea of evolution completely dazzled the presenter, so much so that even the possibility of a creator was completely blotted out. Think also of the great pioneers who discovered the psyche. They began to explain (or explain away) everything in psychological terms. The founder of the counselling movement, Carl Rogers, believed that if we paid attention to our individual psychic healing there would be no more wars. Jung suggested the same. Karl Marx and his followers believed that heaven would inevitably arrive if we bowed down to the outworking of political power. We will go on to see how we have been seduced into thinking that the human mind is the key to all things. Computer technology, evolution, the psyche, political power, the human mind – these are all good and powerful dimensions of creation. But wonder can lead on to idolatry and, as we shall see, idolatry involves sacrifice. The apostle Paul, however, believed that the wonders of creation should lead us on to wonder at the Creator as did the psalmists before him. He wrote: 'Ever since the creation of the world his invisible nature, namely, his eternal power and deity, has been clearly perceived in the things that have been made' (Rom. 1.20).

When we overvalue one aspect of the good creation, other aspects of creation necessarily get undervalued, as on a see-saw: when one thing goes up other things go down. Everything is subjected and even sacrificed to our idol. The theologian Paul Tillich writes about the idolatry of nationalism: 'If a national group makes the life and growth of the nation its *idol*, it demands that all other concerns, economic well-being, health and life, family, aesthetic and cognitive truth, justice and humanity, be sacrificed . . . Everything is centred in the only god, the nation – a god who certainly proves to be a demon.'[3] Gods always demand sacrifice. By sacrificing other good aspects of creation we force them into the shadows. Both Geoffrey and Lynn, whom we talked about in the last chapter, had sacrificed their sexuality for 'higher' moral and ethical values. Their sexuality then plunged into the shadows. We will go on to see how the idolatry of the intellect has pushed many things including sex into the shadows, but first we will look at idolatry from an archetypal point of view.

I have already made the link between archetypes and gods. As I said in the last chapter, Jung believed that the gods of the ancient pagan world were the inner archetypal forces of the psyche projected on to the world outside. Whether the gods are transcendent realties as in the ancient world view or whether they are immanent realties as in the Jungian view, the important thing about the gods is that they pointed to powerful realties of human life. It is a very serious matter that we in our modern folly killed off the gods declaring them to belong to a superstitious world view. We in fact killed off the language only; the archetypal reality now having no way of coming to expression was simply driven into the shadows. The theologian Walter Wink puts it like this:

> The gods, like stars, have been put out of heaven, leaving no light for exploring the darkness. They have become part of the darkness themselves. The gods once named the shapes that come to meet us in the gloom; without them we are pummelled and maddened by forces we have never named and cannot tame. . . . We need the gods back to guide us through this night of history and our own souls.

What is driven into the shadows, unlike sleeping dogs, will not lie. It will find some way of coming to expression. Wink goes on:

> The gods never died, they only became diseases, as Jung put it: 'Zeus no longer rules Olympus but rather the solar plexus, and produces curious specimens for the doctor's consulting room, or disorders the brains of politicians and journalists who unwittingly let loose psychic epidemics on the world.[4]

Without any knowledge of the gods of the psyche we are easy prey for them, for we cannot see their advances before it is too late. We have only to think of our own century and the powers that have unslaved people, such as in religious cults or national militaries, seducing them into committing the most atrocious acts of evil. Or, on a more personal level, as Jung says: 'When, for instance, a highly esteemed professor in his seventies abandons his family and runs off with a young red-headed actress, we know that the gods have claimed another victim.'[5]

As Wink points out, in the Bible the reality of the gods is rarely questioned. The Bible writers believed that the gods were subordinate to Yahweh. 'All gods bow down before him' says the Psalmist in Psalm 97.7. Yahweh is often pictured as presiding over a heavenly council: 'God has taken his place in the divine council; in the midst of the gods he holds judgement.' (Ps. 82.1) The apostle Paul certainly believed in the existence of the gods. 'There are many "gods" and many "lords" . . . .' (1 Cor. 8.5). He also knew their power to enslave. 'Can you turn back again to the weak and beggarly elemental spirits?' he asked the Galatian Christians, incredulous since they had tasted freedom (Gal. 4.9). Indeed, Paul believed that Christ came to defeat the evil powers that imprison us: 'He disarmed the principalities and powers and made a public example of them, triumphing over them' (Col. 2.15).

Without the gods this profound meaning of the cross is all but lost to us. The theologian Gustaf Aulen in his important book *Christus Victor*[6] tells us that the most pervasive view of the early Church was that on the cross of Christ God defeated the powers that enslave us. This biblical understanding of the meaning of Christ's death on the cross has been relegated by the less biblical, 'penal substitution' theory.[7] In order to participate in shadow work we need to engage fully with the truth that Christ defeated the powers that enslave us, for only then can we effectively relativize archetypal power.

Now the implication of the above is that when we raise some aspect of creation to an idolatrous level, we fall into the hands of the gods.[8] In archetypal language, we fall into the grip of an archetype. Jung believed that the Nazi party had fallen into the powerful hands of the warrior god

Wotan. Geoffrey and Lynn of the last chapter and the seventy-year-old professor above had fallen into the hands of Aphrodite. Naming the powers that enslave us is very important in shadow work, as we shall see later, for it brings them out of the shadows and into the light and it is the light that dispels the darkness. It is my belief that our culture has let itself be gripped by Apollo. This is what we will go on to explore. First, however, we need to put the gods in their place.

If the gods of the psyche are real, to pretend they do not exist only forces them into the shadows. From there, one day, they may return. As Sir Laurens van der Post puts it so graphically: 'The dark rejected forces massing in the shadow of the unconscious, as it were, knife in hand, will demand revenge for all that man and his cultures have consciously sacrificed of them.'[9] A biblical faith urges us to have a different attitude to the gods. We are to acknowledge them yet not serve them for they bow the knee to the living God. I have already noted how important faith in God is for shadow work. Walter Wink puts it like this: 'Honour the gods; worship God.' Indeed, as Wink points out, we are to 'order the gods to worship Yahweh'. This is the message of Psalm 29.1–2:

> Ascribe to the Lord, O sons of gods,
>   ascribe to the Lord glory and strength.
> Ascribe to the Lord the glory of his name;
>   worship the Lord in holy array.

'Honour the gods, do not serve them.' Put in a metaphor which is closer to the theme of this book: '. . . it may be our fate to have as our dancing partner for a few spins one of the great gods. But it is still the Fiddler that calls the tunes. The trick is staying in the dance – do not, oh do not let the god escort you off the floor and out into the dark. Stay in close earshot of the music, keep moving with the beat, and the Fiddler will see you through.[10] This fits exactly with what we know of idolatry. We honour the wonders of all created life, but we do not worship any creature. We dance with all of creation as Sophia did at the beginning, but we never let any creature take us out of earshot of the Fiddler. There is something of Sophia in all of the gods. When we dance with the gods we also dance with Sophia. There is something of Folly in all idolatries. Folly is the seductive one. It is she who seeks to lead us astray.

I said earlier that our culture has let itself be gripped by the god Apollo. In Greek mythology, Apollo is the sun god, the god of light. He is also the god of law, order and rationality. To honour Apollo is to praise reason, but to worship Apollo is to fall into the idolatry of reason. Let us first give honour where honour is due.

The faculty of reason is what we call the human intellect. Reasoning, planning, sorting, 'thinking things through', logic, analysis, forming concepts – these are all activities of the intellect. What a remarkable gift it is. It has given us all the wonders of modern science and technology – both are evidence of its power. Indeed, without the gift of the intellect we would not be human. We would not be able to build our buildings, plan and write our books, sort our washing or file our papers. Certainly we would not be able to write books on computers. Some Christian people denigrate the intellect. They see it as a threat to faith. 'Don't go to university. It is the graveyard of Christians,' I have heard people say. Later, we will see how the idolatry of the intellect has indeed been an enemy to Christian faith, but the human mind when seen as a God-given gift is wondrous indeed. I always begin my course in the philosophy of religion with a session 'in praise of reason'.

One of the earliest descriptions of the exercise of the gift of the intellect is the story of Adam naming the animals in the garden of Eden. As we will recall, Adam is part of creation, all of which is declared by God to be 'very good'. Adam is among other things a thinking being. Thus

God affirms the goodness of the human intellect. Adam, as the story goes, 'gave names to all cattle, and to the birds of the air, and to every beast of the field' (Gen. 2.19).[11] It is unlikely that Adam saw a long-legged and long-necked creature and named it 'George', then named the large grey animal with the big ears and long nose 'Freda'. Adam's naming involved analysis, differentiation and the formation of concepts. The first creature parades itself. Adam analyses it, examines its constituent parts: four long legs, long neck, yellow and black in colour. The second creature comes along. Adam differentiates: the legs, neck, size, shape of ears and colour are different from those of the first animal. Adam begins to form concepts or intellectual constructs. He calls one animal 'giraffe', the other 'elephant'. The very diversity of the animal kingdom soon involves Adam in more and more complex and nuanced concepts in this naming process. Concepts or categories of insect, mammal and fish are born in Adam's mind.

The human intellect can also play its part in the healing or redemption of the world. Recently, I was alerted to a story of the healing and saving power of the gift of the intellect. John, a man in his forties, was above average in intelligence. He remembers his schooldays with anger and great sorrow. There he was subjected to humiliation, and bullying by teachers because his words and numbers came out all wrong when he put them down on paper. The emotional trauma of this childhood experience has stayed with him and indeed moulded the subsequent thirty years of his life. John was at school before 'dyslexia' was conceived. This is a wonderfully redemptive concept. 'Naming' this disability meant that other children with a similar problem might be saved from the same kind of destructive experience.

The intellect, truly, is a wonderful gift. However, sadly, as the apostle Paul observes with great insight, 'they exchanged the truth about God for a lie and worshipped and served the creature rather than the Creator, who is blessed for ever! Amen' (Rom. 1.25). Dazzled by the light of reason we began to put the human mind in the place of God. In other words, we let Apollo seduce us and take us away from the dance floor. The Bible tells us that God is faithful – that he will not fail us. We came to believe that reason would not fail us provided that we served it well. Reason, we thought, would determine the truth about the universe. It could even decide whether God exists or not. Since the existence of God cannot be decisively proved, we thought, it is irrational to believe in him. Thus a new religious tradition was born – the tradition of 'rationalism'.

Much is being written about 'rationalism' lately. Most of this is of a highly philosophical nature. Our concern, however, is with the shadow cast by this idolatry and we need to move quickly on. Idolatry, as I have said, is like a seesaw. When one thing goes up, other things go down. When the human mind is elevated to the heavenly realm, what goes down is the body. The body plunges into the shadows. Perhaps nowhere is this more clearly shown than in the following words of the philosopher Plato. Plato was, and probably still is, the most influential philosopher in the Western world. He stands near the beginning of the rationalist tradition: 'So long as we have the body with us in our enquiry, and our soul is mixed up with so great an evil, we shall never attain sufficiently what we desire, and that, we say, is the truth.'[12]

For Plato, the body is a 'hindrance' to the pursuit of truth, even a great 'evil'. When we examine these words carefully not only do we find a severe disparaging of the body, we also notice something else: Plato makes a distinction between the soul and the body. To put it another way: he does not include the body in the 'soul'. The implication is that the body becomes a mere appendage to the self. This has become a pervasive view even up to today.

Recently a friend found she had Menière's disease. This is a disease of the ear which causes severe tinnitus and loss of hearing. The specialist told her coldly that she should consider having an operation. The chances of success, he said, were slim and she might be left stone-deaf, but, he went on, since she had so little hearing left in the one ear it would not matter that much. My friend fought to keep the tears back. This doctor seemed to have no sense that his words were cutting her to her soul. I believe that he shared the idolatrous view expressed by Plato that ears are just a part of the body – a mere appendage. According to this view the body is something we have, not something we are. In desperation my friend sought help from a Buddhist acupuncturist. This woman asked her questions about her life and her feelings with care and sensitivity. She treated her as a whole human being. For her, the soul or self includes the body. I do not wish to idealize Eastern traditions. Yet, in this case, I believe we have much to learn. How ironic that some of my friend's Christian colleagues warned her about the dangers of acupuncture to her soul!

You cannot dance with soulless flesh. The first step to dancing with our shadows then is to re-include our bodies into our soul. Recently, I went to our local swimming pool. I noticed the serious swimmers with their faces set hard, ploughing up and down the pool, having to keep up the record of lengths and timing they had set themselves. I made a point of not joining them. I set myself no task. Instead I focused my attention on bodily awareness – the silky softness of the warm water against my skin. I rolled around on my back, and stared up at the ceiling enjoying the muffled echoey sounds. Then I turned on my front, and hung in the water and sunk slowly. So I reacquainted myself with my body, and as I did so I felt that through the water the benevolent hands of God were holding me. As we shall see later, when we lose our bodies we lose our

God also, for God, as my religion teaches me, comes to me through the flesh (John 1.1). Thomas Moore, in his book *Care of the Soul* advises that we become reacquainted with our bodies by listening to them speak.[13] When our neck plays up we should ask it what is wrong. It may tell us that it is fed up with carrying an anxiety – that a problem has literally become a 'pain in the neck'. We need to recover our lost communication with our bodies and learn once again the language of the body.

When our bodies were driven into the shadows, so were sex, the feminine and feelings. These three are all associated with the body, as we shall see. Much has been written lately about this and I shall be brief. The theologian Origen (*c.* AD 185–254), who was influential in the ancient Christian world, wrote: 'There is a love of the flesh which comes from Satan, and there is also another love, belonging to the spirit, which has its origins in God: and nobody can be possessed by two loves . . . . If you have despised all bodily things . . . then you can acquire spiritual love.' The biblically oriented and great preacher John Chrysostom (d. AD 407) subscribed to the view that before the fall Adam and Eve dwelt in pure virginity with no 'lustfulness' and 'no desire for intercourse.'[14] These two are not isolated voices but are representative of a pervasive anti-sex and anti-body view that has permeated Christianity to our own day.

Those of us who are aware of the danger of pushing God-given gifts into the shadows should not be surprised by stories of sexual misconduct and even perversions. Susan Griffin, in her excellent book *Pornography and Silence*, argues persuasively that hard-core pornography is humiliation and violation of the body and sex. It is, she says, due to men projecting on to women the fear and despising of their own bodies.[15]

A book I recommend on Christian anti-sexual history is James Nelson's *Embodiment*. In a recent conversation I

had with James Nelson, he agreed that the title of his
book still carried with it overtones of the body as appendage, but he is doing much to reintroduce the body as
part of the self. Yet old habits die hard, as the following
story illustrates. Jane had been through a painful divorce.
Later, she found another partner and entered into a committed relationship with him. However, she felt that she
was emotionally unable to go through another public
marriage ceremony at that time. The leaders of her
church discussed her case and decided that she should be
forbidden the Eucharist until she changed this new relationship. One of the leaders who made this decision is a
property developer. He sometimes puts in offers on
houses and withdraws them before there is any signing of
contracts. It is very distressing when you are trying to sell
a house to have the verbal agreement revoked. Appar-
ently, there was no similar discussion in the church about
forbidding him the Eucharist until he changed his behaviour! This story illustrates the pervasive shadow view
that when we think of 'sin' we think of sex. James Nelson
pointed out the hypocrisy in the popular wisdom of our
day: 'Sex is dirty; save it for someone you love!'[16] Behind
this anti-sex view lies the anti-body attitude so strongly
expressed by the philosopher Plato.

The idolatry of the intellect drives the body and sex into
the shadows. It also drives the feminine into the shadows.
Apollo is masculine. The link between sexism and idolatry
of the mind is not quite clear. It seems that men being the
dominant power group simply claimed the intellect as
their own, thus adding 'maleness' to the pantheon of idols.
Women then became identified with the realm of the
body. St Augustine and Thomas Aquinas, two of the most
influential thinkers in the Christian Church, both actually
wondered why God had bothered to create women at all
since they did not have souls! Recently, in a debate about
the use of feminine imagery for God in the Hot House, a

debating forum at the Greenbelt Arts Festival, I heard an argument put forward and maintained by a Christian priest. He said that feminine imagery for God must be rejected on the grounds that it would introduce an erotic element into the Christian faith. For this man at least it appears that women are to be regarded with suspicion since they belong to the realm of the body and sex.

Along with sex and the feminine, feelings and emotions also have fared badly through the soul/body dualism of Plato. They too have been downgraded to the 'body' category. It is this dualism that lurks behind the 'big boys don't cry' ethic we touched on in the last chapter. So little attention has been paid to our emotional life in our education that we have been left virtually alone to sort out matters of the heart. Our schooling has not included discussions about the meaning and place of emotions in life, of love and what to expect when relationships go wrong, or of the range of feelings we might experience following the loss of a loved one. In the Church, emotional needs have been too often spiritualized or moralized. More prayer, devotional life and moral will has been counselled as the cure for many ills, including difficult relationships. In the last chapter I talked of the prostitute who used sex because she wanted to be held. Counsel that focuses on moral effort whilst ignoring the deeper emotional factors at work would do little to help her find life. It would simply compound her misery. Emotions move us to act for or against our moral conscience. Once again I stress that we should not underestimate the power of the psyche here. Only when the prostitute's deep need to be held is met will she be able to make lasting moral decisions.

Today we are seeing a reaction to the undervaluing of feeling life. Some writers are even identifying the 'soul' or 'spirit' as the unconscious. This temptation is understandable and even desirable, for it helps to reinstate emotional life after its long exile in the shadows. In this book I have, and will, refer to work with the unconscious as 'soul' work. However, I think that we should be careful not to tip the see-saw the other way; to downgrade human reason and elevate emotional life.

By putting Apollo in place of God we push God into the shadows. First, as I have noted, we declared that we have no grounds to believe in God because his existence cannot be proved. Second, we banished God from the world and replaced him with Apollo the lawgiver. It happened in this way.

The philosopher Descartes is often called the father of modern philosophy. His famous maxim is *cogito ergo sum* – 'I think therefore I am.' This maxim became the cornerstone for our modern world view. Basically it reasserts the belief of the philosophers of ancient Greece that humans are essentially thinking beings. Descartes once again split human nature in two parts: mind and body. Once again the mind – the real self – was pictured as lodged in an alien body in an alien world. Descartes went on to describe the body in mechanistic terms. He pictured the body and the world as a machine-like entity – working according to fixed mechanical laws. The machine metaphor has undoubtedly served us well. It has given us laws of nature, enabled us to make predictions and indeed has provided the founding insight for modern science – but at a price. A machine world is a lifeless world.

The writer Fritjof Capra puts it like this: 'A living, divine Spirit pervading all of creation can have no place in such a world. A machine working according to fixed laws "has no purpose, life, or spirituality".' Similarly, the writer Karl Stern talks of 'a fearful estrangement'. 'Just think,' he writes, 'of nature as nothing but a huge, vastly extended soulless machine which you can take apart experimentally and analyse mathematically, which you can run, but with which you have lost all oneness!'[17] Was it this view that I saw reflected in the stony faces of the swimmers in the local swimming pool? Were they dragging their bodies through the water under the tyranny of the clock? This loss of spirituality from the world means that we lose God from creation. The most we can do is see God as a machine minder who started the whole thing off and then retreated behind the clouds, only appearing now and again to tinker with the mechanism. How different the world was for the biblical writers: God 'sends his command to the earth; his word runs swiftly. He spreads the snow like wool and scatters the frost like ashes. He hurls down his hail like pebbles' (Ps. 147.15–17).

The Psalmist, it seems, had only to look at the snow and the rain and sense the presence of God calling them into being. God's activity is not confined to the natural world but is seen also in the rise and fall of nations, of rulers, of economic life and of personal relationships. We have already discussed the activity of God in relation to the political programme of Cyrus of Persia. The biblical writers experienced God in every dimension of life, even in the most ordinary event. The apostle Paul, as we saw earlier, experienced the comfort of God in the simple visit of his friend. The biblical writers are not implying pantheism – where God is equated with creation itself. Their perspective is that the presence of God is mediated through the ordinary (as well as through the extraordinary) events in this world. Oh, if we too could once again walk, or dance, with God in this world as did Adam and Eve and the biblical writers. I want to know that the ground holding me is God holding me, that my breathing in is God breathing into me, that God holds me up in the waters of a swimming pool, that God visits me through my friends, or acupuncturists, or Cyrus of Persia!

If we put Apollo the lawgiver in the place of the Creator God, everything about our relationship with God takes a legalistic turn. Sin and repentance, for example, we see solely in terms of a failure to live up to prescribed moral rules. Being a good Christian witness is seen in terms of showing our non-Christian friends how God has enabled us to obey the moral and spiritual laws. John V. Taylor in his book *The Go Between God* notes how quickly Christ became identified with Apollo.[18] As a result Dionysus, the polar opposite of Apollo, was plunged into the shadows. Dionysus is androgynous, embracing female and male energies and when honoured, inspires spontaneity, ecstasy, rock and roll, mystery and tragedy. Dionysus from the shadows inspires joyriding soul-destroying drugs; the drug 'ecstasy' is a Dionysian word that has taken on a shadow character.

When we lose Dionysus we also lose the concept of the holiness of God, or rather, holiness becomes moralized, tamed. 'God is holy' becomes 'God does not break the rules'. But as Rudolph Otto shows us in his book *The Idea of the Holy* holiness is something that causes the tingle down the back of the spine.[19] Holiness describes the God of the great Protestant reformer Martin Luther: 'a moral enigma'; 'beyond good and evil'; 'his ways are inscrutable'; he is a 'terror in the night'. Jung pointed out that in the book of Job God breaks most of the 'rules', including those against theft and even murder! Lose Dionysus and we also lose the wild side of God. The Spirit in the Bible is more like Dionysus than Apollo. The Spirit is feminine, is like the wind, *ruach* in Hebrew; say the word loudly and you begin to get its meaning.[20] Like the wind, and like Dionysus, the Spirit blows where she will (John 3.8). As Taylor implies, Pentecost was much more like a Dionysian party than an Apollonian meeting: 'They are filled with new wine' (Acts 2.13). Dionysus, known as Bacchus to the Romans, is the god of wine. Oh, that we were more orthodoxly Trinitarian in our beliefs engaging with 'the Father' who is the Creator God, who calls us out of the maternal swamp, supports us with his hand and gives us stability and courage; with the Son, the humanity of God embracing body and mind; and with the Spirit, male and female, untamed, wild and holy.

When Christianity is in the grip of Apollo, when the Christian life is characterized by moralism and legalism, there is little wonder that many people will not set foot inside a Christian church; to them Christianity is about guilt, judgement, prescribed behaviour and prescribed belief. A friend of mine was at a party a few weeks ago. For some obscure reason organ music was on the stereo. Someone said, 'It sounds like a church in here,' and someone else said, 'Yes, I'm already beginning to feel guilty.' This impression of Christianity is, sadly, not untypical. I was once invited to speak at a New Age conference in Cambridge. I decided to present the Christian gospel as I understood it. My theme was 'the God of compassion or the God of oppression'. After my talk, a man came up to me and told me how after a failed marriage his church had rejected him. I soon discovered that many people attracted to the New Age movement were 'failed Christians'. They had failed to conform to the ethos of the Church. Yet these people still had a passionate desire for a relationship with God.

Under the influence of Apollo and the idolatry of the intellect, then, Christianity has become excessively moralized and legalized. The result is that both Jesus and his message have been obscured. We have turned him into a moral teacher of timeless truths. People do not go out in droves to hear someone enforcing a new set of rules for them to live by. They flocked to Jesus because he offered them life in the midst of their political and religious oppression. For, at that time too, legalistic moralism was the order of the day. Jesus' harshest criticism was of religious oppressors.

Jesus showed people what the Creator of the universe was really like, a God of compassion, not a God of domination and control: 'I and the Father are one' (John 10.30). Jesus came 'to preach good news to the poor . . . to proclaim release to the captives and recovering of sight to the blind, to set at liberty those who are oppressed' (Luke 4.18). By Jesus' acts of healing, his affirmation of the marginalized and of those who fail to live up to the rules; by his parables of the woman searching and searching for the lost coin and of the shepherd who left ninety-nine sheep to find the one who was lost; by the father who throws his arms around the son who has messed up on life – Jesus showed that God is unconditional love that endlessly reaches out. Others may criticize and condemn for not living up to the rules, but God does not, and never will, no matter how badly we mess up.

Perhaps the most poignant story that illustrates God's unconditional love is what I have called the story of Jesus the cuddler. The Greek word, translated as 'he took them in his arms', means that Jesus cuddled the children. What was Jesus' message? That God has come to pick us up and throw his arms around us. No amount of moralizing would help the prostitute I talked of in the last chapter but Jesus the cuddler will. When it comes to shadow work, as I have noted in the story of Martin, Jesus being the cuddler means that he embraces both the light and the shadow – both the mind and the body, women and men, black and white, heterosexual and homosexual, prostitute, the 'sane' and the psychotic. This gospel is radical indeed.

Persisting in the idolatry of the intellect means that we have lost God from the world outside and that we have obscured the God of compassion in the Church. We have also lost God from our inner world. The Jungian writer Robert Johnson writes: 'In our pride and hubris, our faith in our unassailable reason, we cut ourselves off from our origins in our unconscious and from the deepest parts of ourselves.'[21] When we imagine reality to be a machine, only that which can be quantified and measured may become part of that reality. Soul, spirit, dreams, visions, religious experience – all the ways in which since the beginning we communicated with our God are banished to the realms of meaninglessness and superstition. A couple of years ago I gave a seminar to a Christian audience on the same theme as this book. I made the statement that

God speaks to us through dreams. A man suddenly stood up at the back and accused me of being New Age and unbiblical. He then symbolically strode out. Thankfully someone else came to my aid. This man pointed out that virtually every major turning-point in biblical history came about through a dream. For example, Peter's vision of the sheet lowered from heaven containing the animals (Acts 10.10ff.). This vision was indeed a major turning-point in the history of God's people. It convinced the early Church leaders that Christianity was not just for the Jews.

Under the influence of the idolatry of the mind there is a great reluctance to even take seriously the theme of this book. In order to dance with our shadows we must first accept that there is an unconscious world. Here I believe that Freud and Jung come to us as prophets. These two have particularly opened our eyes to the fact that a whole realm has been sent into exile.

Finally, the idolatry of the mind under Apollo has led to great injustice – to the oppression of minority groups. Apollo has seduced us into thinking that we are objective in our thought. This blinds us to our own biases, insecurities and prejudices. Thus, for example, those who are in the public realm and have access to political power in reality define what being rational is. In short, they rationalize their own beliefs and prejudices, imposing these on everyone. Putting it crassly, those in public power in this part of the world have generally been able-bodied, white, heterosexual and male. The thinking of this group has defined what is rational and what is for the common good. Not only religious believers, but also the ideas and thought of other groups – such as black people, gay people and women – have been relegated from the public arena to the margins of society. Their views have been pushed into the shadows. We are witnessing the struggles that women, gay people and disabled people have in getting their political concerns on the agenda. As I write, an Act of

Parliament is being discussed that appears to deny travellers the right to their particular lifestyle. Their claims are seen as unreasonable.

The most poignant story concerning marginalization came to my ears recently at a Hot House debate at the Greenbelt Festival. A young man told how he was diagnosed as mentally ill. He pointed out how in our society mentally ill people are defined as irrational (in keeping, of course, with the above argument). He was sectioned – that word again! In hospital different psychiatrists tried to diagnose him in order to determine an appropriate course of medication. This young man bravely and consistently resisted the (rational) categories he was being forced into – schizophrenic, borderline, etc. Finally he was put in a therapeutic group of others who did not fit the categories – all the marginalized within the hospital. Although the behaviour of some of these people was quite extraordinary and worrying, this young man described his experience there as true community!

In this chapter we have seen, then, that the idolatry of the intellect has cast a mighty shadow over the land. Like Sleeping Beauty we have been held in its paralysing grip for 'a hundred years'. The tale also tells us that many princes came to break the spell and failed but when the time had come the thorns parted and a prince walked effortlessly through. With a kiss he wakened the princess and gradually the land stirred into life. There are many signs that we are everywhere waking up from being under the spell of the idolatry of the intellect. There are many signs that Sophia is coming: the books alerting us to the over-commitment to reason, the explosion of interest in emotional life, the rediscovery of the feminine, the return to the body and so on. This presents us with new possibilities and responsibilities. After we have finished rubbing our eyes, we need to re-engage our shadow. This is the concern of the second half of this book.

5 *Shrinking Violets*

There are many things that make us reluctant to step on to the dance floor to dance with our shadow. It is crucial in shadow work to be honest with ourselves. We always start from where we are. I have already addressed some of the things that may tempt us to stay a wallflower: suspicion of Jung; the denigration of emotional or inner life; a moralism that seeks to answer life's problems by moral will alone. There are others: a belief that the focus on self entailed in shadow work is self-indulgence, for example.

There is a poster outside a church near here which says: 'Jesus first; Others second; Yourself last'. This hierarchical arrangement, if taken seriously as an ethic, can be disastrous. I am currently working with someone who in mid-life is trying to deal with great emotional distress. Over the weeks it has emerged that he had a very religious upbringing. As long as he could remember his parents had instilled in him that he should put others before himself. He had few toys of his own as a child. Once, when he went to hospital for a long period, he found in the hospital toy cupboard an old teddy bear with one leg, one ear and an eye hanging lose. He and his bear became inseparable. When eventually he was sent home, his mother took the teddy bear from him and said, no doubt with the noblest of intentions, that God would be happy if he gave away the teddy bear to someone less fortunate than himself. Part of the distress that this man now suffers is guilt because he finds himself obsessively demanding attention. No wonder! We need positive affirmation throughout all stages of our emotional life. If we are deprived of this we become what is known as self-centred. We hang on to what we have, even grab for what we can, for fear that our needs will never be met. To seek a way forward for our lives by engaging in shadow work is not self-centredness but a way out of self-centredness.[1]

Fear is a powerful emotion that keeps us away from shadow work. I have already recounted the words of the gay man: 'I was that person my mother had always warned me about!' These words capture so well the kind of feelings we often have to face when we begin to encounter our shadow. There is an old fairy tale known as 'The Three Golden Hairs'. A young man falls in love with a beautiful princess. He asks the king for his daughter's hand in marriage. The king says, 'Only when you have brought me three golden hairs from the head of the devil will you be old enough to marry my daughter.' The profound psychological truth here is that growth to maturity is by way of a close encounter with our shadow. The tale also captures the intensity with which we may dismiss parts of ourselves. We may fear that our shadow is the very devil himself.

We may also fear the pain of shadow work. Shadow work for the man mentioned above with the teddy bear is involving him in facing the pain he was unable to cope with as a small deprived child. Facing the pain of grief, of robbed childhood, and speaking, or drawing, or painting from out of that pain is often a crucial aspect of shadow work, as we shall see.

For all these reasons and more we may wish to stay off the dance floor, but there is a price to pay for being a wallflower. In order to understand this we need to look at Jung's theory of projection. Projection, as the word implies, occurs when the disowned shadow is projected on to the world outside, just as a movie is projected on to the cinema screen. From there it may lead us a sorry dance. I have already talked about how the shadow of the West is projected on to its enemies. Our personal shadows can also give us the run-around. Again, I have already noted how a man may project the image of a bad mother on to women in his adult life. Many couples in fact fall into a relationship that is made not in heaven, but in the shadows. The man unconsciously projects on to his partner a devouring mother who stares back at him from out of her eyes. He finds that he recoils from intimacy. He begins to stay longer 'at the office'. He wonders whether he has fallen out of love. Eventually he may fall in love with another woman. While his projected shadow parasitically clings to his former partner he feels free with the new woman. He decides to leave and sets up home with her. The trouble is – so does his shadow. For a while there is a honeymoon shadow-free period, but gradually the shadow seeps through the small cracks, through a word here, a look there, almost undetectably until it has pervaded the whole house just as before.

Of course shadow projection is rarely, if ever, just a one-way affair. Projections need hooks – if we may pardon the odd metaphor. Perhaps the women in the life of the man above are also unconsciously looking for a partner who will be to them the father or mother they never had. They begin to nag him for failing to care for them. This drives him further away, until both partners find they are caught in a seemingly hopeless downward spiral. Here the dance is not between ego and shadow but between shadow and shadow; both egos are whirled around helplessly in a shadow dance between shadow partners. As we will go on to see, the kind of dancing we need to do is between the ego and the unconscious. It is a dance of mutuality; first the one partner takes the lead and then the other. When we disown and project our shadow outside ourselves, the dance is not mutual. The shadow has all the initiative.

Often, we can detect our own shadow in the things that we hate most in others. We may, for example, detest with a passion any form of controlling, bossy behaviour. We say that we will never be like that. On the surface we appear to be accepting and non-judgemental. Yet while we are at the front door we have not noticed what is going on in the back of the house. There in the shadows is amassing an intolerance that has not yet found a host. This is projected on to the other from whose face it stares back at us.

It is a very serious matter when those who have not engaged in any shadow work get into a position of power. They may manipulate or oppress others dreadfully from the shadows. It is very likely that the church leaders in the example I gave earlier – of the woman who was refused the Eucharist while she remained in an unacceptable relationship – had not owned their own sexual shadow. This shadow is made even stronger through the collective rejection of sexuality that we have talked about.

We see then that projection of the shadow harms ourselves and it harms others. These words of Jesus are about projection: 'Why do you see the speck that is in your brother's eye, but do not notice the log that is in your own eye? . . . . First take the log out of your own eye, and then you will see clearly to take the speck out of your brother's eye' (Matt. 7.3–5). This, I believe, is an invitation to engage in shadow work. Dancing with the shadow is about taking the log out of our own eye.

There is another price we pay for not dancing with the shadow. When we leave a part of ourselves in the shadows, we are only part alive. The second-century Bishop of Lyons, Irenaeus, said, 'The glory of God is humanity fully alive.' Jung believed that the archetypal symbol for wholeness is a circle. Often in fairy tales the symbol takes the form of a golden ball. Typically this falls down a well to be retrieved by a frog. Frogs were thought of as despicable creatures and were associated with witches' brew and the like – that is with the rejected shadowy world. Such tales point us to the truth that gold is buried with our shadows. It has been all but obscured by the distortions of repression, yet gold it surely is. Perhaps when we unearth our own Apollonian legalistic shadow we will find the gold of peace and order. Apollo served leads to oppression. Apollo honoured as lawgiver brings order, stability, safety and peace, precious gifts in a world that often seems chaotic and disordered. Perhaps in our repressed sexuality there is

a buried seed that once let out begins to colour all of life
with joy and sensuality and sometimes ecstasy.

When we find our shadow, we also find Sophia, the
Wisdom of God. As we have noted, our shadow is made up
of what we disapprove of, not what God disapproves of,
even though we try to drag God over to our way of thinking. Sophia is at the very heart of creation. She was there
with God at the beginning. She is the foundational structure of creation itself. She is the archetype of creation.
When we force aspects of our God-given humanity into
the shadows, we force Sophia off the streets and into the
basement. Like Cinderella there she stays out of sight,
shabby amongst the cinders. One day she may magically
appear upstairs in the ballroom. If we once catch a glimpse
of her beauty we will search and search until we find her,
like the shepherd and his lost sheep.

The invitation then is to dance with the shadow. As we
have seen, this dance is one of mutuality between both
partners – the ego and the shadow. We must also be aware
that our shadow dancing partners are strange and many.
We may find ourselves dancing with the young baby who
feels unwanted, or who feels that her needs will never be
met, or who feels guilty for needing at all. We may find
ourselves dancing with the toddler who is afraid of step-
ping out and taking initiative for fear of being shamed, or
with the one who is embarrassed about his bodily presence. We may find ourselves dancing with the young teenager who was ridiculed at school. 'It may *even* be our fate to
have as our dancing partner for a few spins one of the great
gods,' as Walter Wink puts it.[2]

Dancing with the shadow will also involve us in a
dance of feeling and imagination. The unconscious
seems more happy with the non-rational world of images,
metaphors and symbols. This is perhaps in reaction to the
ego that has been for so long held in the grip of Apollo
and rationalism. Already we have used a number of

different metaphors to gain an understanding of this work: dancing, shadow, gold . . . . We have touched on the imaginative world of Greek myth and we will go on to explore fairy tales and dreams. Our Apollonian side may find this mixing of metaphors and images offensive. That is how it is in this kind of work. The soul (another metaphor!) does not seem to be too bothered about the scruples of our egos. When a man told me he felt embarrassed about the sexist content of his dream I had to tell him that the soul is not always politically correct! Nor is it always logically correct; nor is it always aesthetically correct – by ego standards. I do not mean to say that we should suspend all the sensitivities of our ego – then dance would not be mutual – just that we should refrain from being too hasty with their imposition. For this reason, I have not set out step by step logical instructions on how to dance with the shadow. Instead I offer a series of suggestions, images and metaphors. We are all so different; what will resonate with one person will not resonate with another. Each of us then must find a way forward in this work in dialogue with our own soul.

6 The Ego, the Shadow and the Committee

I have found one metaphor particularly illuminating for shadow work. It captures well much of what we have said above: the plurality of the shadow, the relationship between the ego and the shadow, the way we may integrate the shadow into conscious life and so move forward. I would like to spend some time exploring this metaphor. It asks us to think of the psyche as though it were a committee. The ego is the chairperson of this committee of the soul. It sits at the head of the table. The shadow is composed of all the committee members. They sit around both sides of the table. Now consider a well-run committee. A well-run committee has the chairperson firmly taking the lead and making final strategic decisions, yet only after consulting all the committee members. A badly run committee, on the other hand, has a weak chairperson who is given the run-around by various committee members, or else has his or her ear bent by only one or two committee members. Other members, seeing the favouritism, rebel. In the same way, a badly run psyche does not see the ego firmly taking the lead. The ego gets kicked out of the chairperson's chair and watches on helplessly as first one shadow person and then another takes over the chair and dominates the psyche. Sometimes there is virtual anarchy in the psyche. When this happens we are in complete despair – we feel at our wits' end – we just do not know what to do for the best.

Take Martin, for example. Two of his psyche's committee members are bad child and good child. They sit either side of the table. First, bad child kicks Martin's ego out of the chair and runs things for a while. Then good child kicks bad child out of the chair and pervades the whole committee room with a sense of guilt. Bad child resents being 'put down' and once more kicks good child out of the chair. But where, we may ask, is Martin's ego in all this? Martin's ego is standing by helplessly watching, powerless to take control of the situation. First his ego is persuaded by one committee member, then by the other. It is a very similar situation with Geoffrey. First his ego was whisked away by Aphrodite, then by Hera, then by Aphrodite again. Then perhaps the infant who feels that his needs will never be met pervades the whole psyche with wall-to-wall, 360-degree despair. The task, then, for both Martin and Geoffrey is for the ego to take back the chair and bring some order into a very anarchistic shadow committee.

A bad chairperson is not only one who is weak, but also one who is domineering. A domineering chairperson does not consult her committee members but makes decisions on her own. She especially tries to silence the most awkward members. By suppressing the feelings that emanate from these members the domineering chairperson mistakenly believes she will stay strong and in control. She pays a great price for this, for she ends up with a committee that is only half functioning and a life which is only half lived. As we have said, there is gold in the shadow. Also, very probably, there will come the time when those members of the committee that have been sat upon will in desperation rebel, spewing their sap all over 'the dressed-up dining rooms of strangers'[1]. Remember the words of Geoffrey: 'I have always been in control!'

A chairperson is only as good as the committee members. A domineering chairperson will not get the cooperation he or she needs. She must also treat all committee members equitably, not siding with one against another. As we have seen, this is often very difficult because it means that we have to face and own the awkward parts of ourselves. I am working with a young married couple. When I first saw them, the husband was caught between two women. So ashamed and terrified was he of his behaviour that it took several sessions for him to confess that he had had an affair. He kept assuring me that it was over.

It took several more sessions for him to admit that the affair was not over. He had tried to 'sit on' a part of himself, to hide it from everyone – his wife, his counsellor and himself. A good chairperson must allow on to the committee all the members. He must give them a place, but first he must get to know who they are.

The first stage in dancing with the shadow – to pick up our original metaphor – is to get to know the names of our dancing partners. Using our committee metaphor, we must get to know the names of the committee members. This often involves a great deal of struggle, for it means that we have to face those parts of ourselves that we would rather were not there. That is, of course, why they are in the shadows. I am reminded of the biblical story of Jacob who wrestles with the angel of God. After wrestling with God all night, Jacob asks the angel to bless him. 'What is your name?' asks the angel repeatedly of the struggling Jacob. Only when Jacob reveals his name does the angel bless him (Gen. 32.33–32). Only when the struggling was over and he could say who he really was did the married man mentioned above receive a blessing: 'I am the one who is having an affair.' Yet only when he was sure that he would not be rejected dared he confess. Sitting on God's knee with God's arms around us, knowing that nothing can separate us from the love of God, only then do we dare say who we really are.

How do we get to know our committee members? We get to know them by inviting them to tell us their stories. This story-telling may take many different forms and we will go on later to explore some of these. It is crucial in this work that the story is told from the heart. We invite the committee members to speak out of their feelings. Sometimes their tale needs to be told many times, each time with a different nuance. The story of 'the one who is having an affair', we found, involves a tale of rejection by mother and tyrannical control by father. The ego of this poor man was in the grip of the one who felt that he never measured up. The unhappy relationship he had with his wife was characterized by the feeling that he was always in the wrong: if only he talked about his feelings with her; if only he was more caring; if only he was not so miserable; if only he had not had an affair; if only . . . then they would not be in this mess. He who initially named himself as the 'one who is having an affair' changed and deepened into 'the one who does not measure up'. That is how it is in shadow work. We are always open and responsive to the changes that go on in the shadows.

Freud once said that our latest insight is our next defence. Unconsciously we often try to defend ourselves from the pain of further self-revelation. When we think that we have understood ourselves – named our committee members – we are in danger of not being open to further revelations from the unconscious. The 'one who does not measure up' sat in the chairperson's seat of his psyche's committee most of the time, and especially when he was at home with his wife. Little wonder then that when another woman opened her heart and arms to him unconditionally in total emotional and bodily affirmation – or so it seemed – the 'one who does not measure up' felt such a surge of longed-for well-being and ecstasy that he was powerless to resist. Aphrodite descended and in enchanted fascination he was taken off the dance floor with his ego trotting along behind. After much work in counselling, both partners came to realize what had been going on in the shadows of their relationship. They gradually found they were able to be more accepting of themselves and each other and that they did not have to hide parts of themselves away. Sophia and Aphrodite appeared more frequently in their relationship enabling them to become playmates and lovers. This was a great joy to them because they also realized that they loved each other deeply.

The main aim, then, is to bring into conscious awareness our deepest feelings – to let our committee members tell their story. At every stage on the way we must hold back from clever theoretical analysis of what is going on. 'I feel needy. Oh, that must mean that I had a trauma at the oral stage of development' might be a tempting response to a feeling but it is too controlled, too dominated by the ego. The key to the art of shadow work is to wait upon and listen to the feelings that stir in the unconscious, inviting them to speak.

Often we find that we have only the dimmest sense of a committee member. We find it impossible to name them or to listen to their story, so far are they submerged in the unconscious. Then we may have to go fishing. The psychologist Eugene Gendlin helps us with this.[2] Gendlin has coined the phrase 'felt sense' for what needs to happen here. The phrase 'felt sense' brings in an important aspect of soul work: the body. We try to listen to the language and wisdom of the body. Emotions always seem to have a bodily location; they are in the stomach, or in the back, or in the shoulders, or in the genitals. In fishing for committee members, then, we first try to get the bodily location of a feeling.

Feelings bubble up to consciousness through symbols. Symbols may take the form of either words or images. The second stage is to locate the image or word that is hovering in the depths of the soul. Again, we must stress that this process happens from the bottom up – we let the feeling give us the word or image. We do not impose one from the top. At first the image or word may be very primitive. Gendlin calls this a 'quality-word'. It may be a word 'like tight, sticky, scary, stuck, heavy, jumpy'.[3] This primitive word may then develop into a more sophisticated image or picture. The picture or image may be quite surprising and unexpected. It may come into our awareness sideways on, so to speak. We must be careful not to dismiss an image as irrelevant, or not significant enough. This is the ego wanting to take control again.

Very recently, I engaged in this process myself. I was feeling quite pressurized by a number of things, not the least of which was meeting the deadline for the completion of this book. I also had to do a presentation for some senior managers regarding some consultancy work I had done for them. This was a new area for me and I was feeling nervous. I was beginning to run around like a headless chicken. It was as though my ego had been cut adrift from its moorings in the depths of the unconscious. With great effort, I decided to stop and engage in some shadow work. I lay on my bed and tried to relax. I took some deep breaths and focused on the feelings I had in my body. I located the feeling in the pit of my stomach. I let a word come. The word was 'prickly'. It also felt like there was something undigested in my stomach. Suddenly, as if from nowhere, an image of a hedgehog came into my mind. At first I wanted to dismiss this image as mere superficial word association with 'prickly', but then I realized that this image fitted perfectly – I had an undigested hedgehog in my stomach!

The next stage in engaging the unconscious is to enter into dialogue with the image. First we ask a question like Who are you? or Where have you come from? or What is it that you want? or How old are you? and we wait for the answer. I asked my hedgehog: 'Why are you a hedgehog?' The answer came into my head that it was a hedgehog because it was shy, at times it was even frightened. Then it curled up into a ball and stuck its prickles out in defence. I realized that I had been quite short-tempered or 'prickly' with friends and family lately. I told the hedgehog that I would quite like it to move out of my stomach. At this suggestion, I definitely felt it flinch, curl up and stay put – I had felt its fear. At this stage I finished my shadow work. I had discovered another committee member – 'Prickly the hedgehog' – who had been unconsciously dominating things for quite a long time. I have already said what strange people we find on the committees of our psyche! I have sensed the presence of my hedgehog – its prickliness and its fear – several times since this occasion. I know I have to go back and enter into further dialogue with this committee member. I need to enquire all about the fear that is there; how I can lead it out of my stomach into the world outside; how I can reassure it that it does not need to run back terrified. This may involve me in touching the depths of some very early traumatic experience. I need to hear the hedgehog's story.

Although it feels like 'wall-to-wall hedgehog', although my ego feels powerless to regain the chair of my committee, I am beginning to take distance from the feeling. The tiniest seed of ego authority is beginning to emerge. Like the grain of mustard seed this will grow into a big tree. The ego taking back the chair always begins by conscious recognition of a committee member and by separating oneself out – I have a prickly scared hedgehog; I am not that prickly scared hedgehog.

Further work with my hedgehog, or further dancing with my hedgehog, may take a variety of forms. I may decide to draw it or paint it; I may decide to make it out of clay; I may go into town and buy a toy hedgehog. I have a friend who works as a psychotherapist. She uses a sandbox. This is a six-inch-high, three-foot-by-two-foot box full of sand. She has a shelf of objects and toys – animals, monsters, doll's house furniture, trees, pebbles and so on. She invites her clients to express themselves by creating pictures in the sand with all the various objects.

All these are ways to invite our committee members to tell their story. It is important that we discover what suits our soul here – domination from the top will not do. I have found that this can be very different for different people. What works for one does not work for another. It is quite a crucial stage in soul work when our soul does find a voice. I worked for many months with one young woman. I talked to her all about committees of the psyche and archetypal power. I suggested that she draw her feelings. I even suggested she draw a picture of her committee with all its members. Although she did all these things they seemed to lack depth and authenticity. One day she brought in a tape of the music of Mendelssohn. This was a turning point for her. I went and got a tape recorder and we spent the next few sessions listening to Mendelssohn. She sobbed her way through much of the music. Its ebb and flow seemed to engage the ebb and flow of her own life story. 'This is where I reached the depths of despair', 'This is where I saw a glimmer of hope' and so on. Her soul had found its voice.

Finding the space for soul work is also a matter of waiting upon the soul. If the ego decides that it is going to give two hours per week for soul work without consulting the committee members of the soul, the plan will be sabotaged from the start. Again, we are all very different here. One Christian woman I know has made a sacred shrine in a corner of her bedroom. She has a small table with a crucifix on it and two candlesticks. She has a writing book on the table which is the book of the journey of her soul. Two or three evenings a week she lights the candles, quietens herself and waits upon God. She then picks up her book and either writes or draws or paints whatever comes. Normally she is a very tidy person. She felt that it suited her soul better to be messy and spontaneous in her journal. She draws upside down, writes sideways and splodges paint about.

I am much less formal about my soul work. Sometimes when I am sitting at my computer I will notice that something is bothering me. I grab a piece of paper, draw a line down the middle and engage in dialogue with myself. One conversation went like this:

Ego:	Committee Member:
Who are you?	'The dull one.'
Why are you so dull?	(irritatedly) 'That's just who I am . . . I'm bored.'
Is there nothing I can do? You're taking over everything.	'Then give me something interesting to do.'
But you drag your feet over everything I suggest.	'I want a house to do up.'
That's not possible right now. We have to wait a while. Would it help if we were a little creative here?	'Yes, let's think up some ideas.'
How about fixing up that old pine table?	'When?'
At the weekend.	'OK . . . don't forget.'
I won't forget.	

After this conversation the disturbing feeling began to dissipate.

Making things, restoring old furniture, building work – all these things I enjoy, especially renovating old houses, which I have done several times now. The above conversation revealed to me how much this is a part of who I am. It is a part of myself that must be honoured. It goes very deep; there is almost something instinctual about the urge to renovate houses – a nest-building instinct, maybe. If this 'committee member' is not being honoured – not being allowed to express itself – from the shadows he pervades all of life with a dullness. I have now learned the meaning of that feeling – that I am not honouring a part of myself.

The above conversation also illustrates the important aspect of mutuality in soul work. Often we have to reach a compromise. The ego chairperson does not bully the creative nest-builder into silence, nor does he let him have total control. Together they reach a compromise that satisfies them both.

The conversation is also one which both contained revelation and led to a happy conclusion. This was because the creative nest-builder lay just below the surface of consciousness. My ego did not find him a great threat to the status quo of conscious life. It is much more difficult to engage in a conscious dialogue with a part of ourselves that is a threat to our ego life. Take the man above who was caught between two women, for example. The dialogue he had with himself was much more painful, traumatic and difficult. By inviting the committee member who was having the affair to speak he had to face near anarchy of different feelings – of fear, guilt, disapproval and so on. Sometimes our ego is hardly capable of bringing sufficient order even to begin this type of conversation. Yet we can simply let the different feelings have their say, writing them down or rather writing out of them as they in turn force their way into consciousness. At this stage this is all that is necessary: the different parts of ourselves simply need to know that they are being heard, that they are being given space. Forcing some kind of compromise at this stage would again be inauthentic – an imposition from above.

Sometimes in effective soul work there is no great revelation. It is enough just to allow some feeling to come to expression without trying to name it or even trying to crystallize it into an image. Once I was trying to write. I had the pressure of a deadline. I just could not seem to get on. My mind constantly kept wandering. It was as though a great obstacle was in the way. I found a piece of paper and some crayons and drew a river with me in a canoe going up it. Either side on the banks I drew houses. All of them had their backs to the river. None of them had any windows facing the river. The scene was solitary and it invoked a slight feeling of loneliness in me. This took me about ten minutes. It was the most primitive of sketches. By artistic standards it was embarrassing, but drawing and painting in soul work is not aesthetically qualified. We are not interested in producing artistic masterpieces. I did not have any great revelations about my shadow nor did I reach any conclusions about how I should change my behaviour. All I know is that the mood had lifted and I was able to get on with my work.

Writing, painting, sand play – all these activities are ways in which the ego can get to know and enter into a relationship with the shadow. It is very important that the initiative in this work comes from above the border or membrane. It is a different matter altogether to engage in this kind of work from below the border. If we have fallen into psychosis, the above activities may draw us further into the shadowy archetypal world where we become fascinated with the numinous power of the images. Great works of genius may come from below the border, but there is a price to pay. We have only to think of the artist Van Gogh to know that this is so. If we are unfortunate enough to experience bouts of psychosis, maybe the best way of managing them is to try to do as many normal everyday things as possible – do the washing-up, dig the garden, spring-clean the house . . . . Often we simply have to wait until we reappear above the border. Sadly, then we have to face the mess that we may have made. From below the border, in our paranoia and sense of omnipotence, we can do many impulsive things: have our phones disconnected, resign from our jobs, bully our friends, and so on.

The more we get to know our committee members, the more we may anticipate how they will behave in certain situations. Then the better able we will be to manage our feelings. Earlier I mentioned that some time ago I had to present a research report before some senior managers. I knew that I was in danger: my ego could easily be dislodged when the time came to face them. A small boy in short trousers could easily jump into the ego's chair and project the critical teacher on to them all. Indeed, when I thought about the coming meeting I could already feel him stirring. The temptation was to not think about it. Yet I knew that way lay danger because not thinking about it also meant not preparing properly and, in a self-fulfilling prophecy, I would behave like a school boy who had not done his homework properly. I negotiated with the small boy in me. I became aware that he was really terrified of being humiliated. I promised that I would not leave a stone unturned in my preparation. I also promised that I would have a trial run-through on the morning before I was to give my report. This would minimize the chance of humiliation. I did all these things. The trial run-through, which I did before a friend, also had another important purpose: it allowed me to experience all the shadow feelings in a safe, contained way and come to terms with them before the actual event. It worked. The small boy behaved himself. In fact, I found the danger went the other way. In the actual meeting I found that at times I was in danger of being over-confident; ego inflated. Next time, I will need to engage with this committee member also.

In his book *Owning Your Own Shadow* the Jungian analyst Robert Johnson also points out the importance of shadow rehearsals, or rituals, as he calls them. He goes so far as to say that the unconscious cannot tell the difference between a ritual and actual reality. He recounts a shadow ritual of a couple on the night before their wedding.

They held a ritual where they made their 'shadow vows'. The groom said, 'I will give you an identity and make the world see you as an extension of myself.' The bride replied, 'I will be compliant and sweet but underneath I will have the real control. If anything goes wrong, I will take your money and your house.' They then drank champagne and laughed heartily at their foibles, knowing that in the course of their marriage, these shadow figures would inevitably come out. They were ahead of the game because they had recognised the shadow and unmasked it.[4]

Sometimes in the press of life we may want quickly to hold impromptu committee meetings. We are faced with a decision we have to make on the spot or we are confronted by a situation that is emotionally difficult for us. The psyche feels as though it may degenerate into anarchy as first one member then another tries to get the chair. The better we know our committee members and the more of them we know, the more able we are to take control of the situation. Sometimes we have to be quite forceful in bringing about psychic discipline. We are confronted with a certain situation and we feel insecure; maybe somebody says something to us and we feel humiliated. We sense the hurt child in us trying to take over the chair. We may have to say firmly: 'I feel your pain but I am not letting you into the chair. We will sort this out later.' It is essential that we are true to our word here. If we fail to keep our word, this is tantamount to bullying suppression and, as we have seen, no committee member will stand for this for long. We make space later in the day to engage with the hurt child, either by dialogue, or by painting or whatever.

How we work with the soul, then, is a very personal matter. Indeed, some people find it tremendously difficult to engage in soul work for themselves. Thankfully, the view is disappearing that you only go to see a counsellor or psychotherapist when you are emotionally sick. A once-a-week session, or once a fortnight with a therapist or counsellor is a time for many people to engage in soul work. The counselling room is their sacred space. There, with their counsellor as soul partner, they can pay attention to their otherwise neglected soul. Many people criticize such a thing as self-indulgent, as we have already discussed. We live in a crazy world, one in which it is entirely acceptable to pay attention to the car and to get it serviced regularly, in which it is appropriate to visit the dentist or the optician for regular check-ups. So why not regular, preventative care of the soul?

There are times in life when we feel particularly desperate, when we feel alone and hopeless. Shadow work seems only to reinforce the feeling that nothing will ever change. At such times we need assurance that we are not lost in totally alien world. Then we need an archetypal perspective and we turn to this next.

7 *Fairy Tales and Dreams*

As we have seen, Jung believed that we may discern archetypal patterns or themes in fairy tales and dreams. I believe we need to be cautious here. Some people treat fairy tales as though they were on the level of Scripture. I believe this is a mistake. Scripture is the ultimate reference for the meaning of our lives. Scripture tells us directly about God, the origin and destiny of human life, evil and how evil is finally overcome. In short, Scripture is theologically qualified. Fairy tales, on the other hand, are psychologically qualified. They do not give us guidance in the ultimate mysteries of life. They tell us about patterns we may find in the psychic dimension of life, as we shall see. It may help to compare this confusion with another more common one we often make – a confusion between science and religion. Some people think that science and religion are in direct conflict with each other. They want to put evolution or the 'big bang' over against creation. Others argue whether the six days of creation accord with the latest scientific theory of the origins of the universe. Here again we have confusion between the function of scientific theories and Scripture. Science and Scripture, like fairy tales and Scripture, serve different purposes. The creation story tells us about the ultimate meaning of life. The natural sciences tell us about the biological or physical structure of life.

In order to see how we may go about discerning psychological archetypal patterns we will first examine a fairy tale. Then we will go on to look at dreams. I have chosen the story of Sleeping Beauty or Brier Rose as it is familiar to most of us. The tale begins with the king and queen, who have no child. In this kind of work we explore each symbol as though handling a precious object in the dark. We turn it over in our hands and let our fingers trace its contours until it reveals its meaning. Kings, queens and kingdoms are to do with political rule. This is rule from the top. It is about the status quo. The psychological symbol of the king is also about rule from the top, from the ego. It is about what currently makes up our conscious life. The tale of Sleeping Beauty tells us of barrenness. There is no child, no new birth, no successor to the throne. Often we feel that our lives are lacklustre. They are uncreative and seem to be going nowhere. We are on a treadmill. We lack energy. May be we feel dreadfully depressed.

A frog appears to the queen as she is bathing and announces that she will have a child. Frogs, as I have said, come from below, from the bowels of the earth, from water, from wells, from the unconscious and the realm of instinct. Water is well known as an archetypal symbol for the unconscious. This part of the tale sounds like a perverse annunciation story until we remember that wisdom too is found in this realm (Job 39.13ff.). Our Christmas cards portray the angel Gabriel as ethereal, hovering in the air, feet off the ground. This image does not come from the biblical story. Perhaps these cards show up our Platonic world view, where the holy is that which has the least involvement with matter. If we are alert, when life seems to have stood still for a long while, something may suddenly turn up – something that we may be inclined to reject as distasteful. The appearance of this messenger from the depths may herald an approaching change.

The child is born. She is beautiful. There is great rejoicing. A feast is held, but in this impoverished kingdom there are only enough golden plates for twelve fairies. The thirteenth fairy is not invited. Psychologically, although something has shifted, a major change has come about, a part of the soul has been left in the shadows. As we have said many times in different words, when a part of ourselves is rejected and pushed into the shadows it exerts from there a destructive influence on our behaviour. The thirteenth fairy, in her indignation, casts a spell over the princess. Thirteen is an important symbolic number. Twelve is the number of completeness and inclusion. We may imagine our conscious life bounded by a circle with twelve points. Often the boundaries of our ego kingdom are quite small and mean. Our lives are dull, barren and lacklustre. We have no room for thirteen; she is not included. Archetypal symbols may apply to outer communal life as well as personal inner life. In all groups and organizations a thirteen will emerge. Thirteens are the heretics, the ones who do not fit, the awkward ones. Twelves are often tempted to push them out, but thirteens are like the grit in the oyster. Without the heretics the Church will not produce any new pearls. Without the awkward ones any organization will become barren.

From the shadows 'thirteen' casts her spell. The king hides the spinning-wheels. When we get in the grip of an archetype we feel as though we are under a spell. No matter what we do we cannot get free. It is as though we are caught in an old pattern of behaviour. We crumple with embarrassment and feelings of inadequacy every time a certain person comes along. We feel pessimistic about everything even when things are going well. With great heroic acts of ego-will we try to keep down the shadow and overcome its spell – all to no avail. This king tries to suppress the imagination. Spinning is about fantasy, and dreaming – we spin yarns. But when the child reaches adulthood and womanhood she sets off exploring the castle. In her innocence, she falls into the hands of 'thirteen'. She has become fascinated by an archetype. She has been led off the dance floor. She pricks her finger and the spell becomes effective. This happens when the king is not at home watching over his daughter. Suppression is hard. We cannot keep it up all the time. One day when we are distracted by our ego affairs the shadow does its work.[1]

The princess, and all the realm with her, fall under the spell – a sleep of a hundred years. Once again conscious life becomes barren, is ineffective, is going nowhere. The birth of the new princess that promised so much comes to nought. This is how it is for us at times. One step forward and two steps backward. During that time many princes try to break through the briers that surround the castle, but are choked to death by the thorns. Again we make great moral efforts to pull ourselves together, to snap out of it, but once again to no avail. Only when the hundred years are up is one prince successful. Effortlessly he walks through the thorns that part before him.

In English we have only one word for 'time'. In the greek language there are two words, *chronos* and *kairos*. *Kairos* means something like 'the right time'. This word refers to the coming of the messiah, when the time was right the messiah was born. In shadow work, the concept of the *kairos* is very important. We may find that we are caught in the grip of a depression that is never-ending. No matter what we do it will not lift. It is as though we are under a spell. Some people in this condition go from counsellor to counsellor for help or they may think that their depression has a biological cause; they go to the doctor for pills or to acupuncturists and homeopaths. Some travel miles to a Christian group because well-meaning people have told them that they need deliverance from demonic oppression. Like the prince saviours who fail in the fairy tales, nothing seems to work. The distress seems to last for ever – 'a hundred years'. Many times they say they cannot possibly go on any more. But one day, sometimes suddenly and miraculously, the depression lifts. With other people, the depression does not lift all at once, but gradually. In both cases the *kairos* has come; it is the right time.

Waiting for the *kairos* is often an essential part of shadow work. It calls for, and forges, faith, hope, patience and endurance – the gifts of the Spirit that the apostle Paul talks about (Gal. 5.22). When a person is in psychological distress it is not only themselves but all those around them who seem to be caught in the spell. We are all called upon to develop and forge these gifts. Many times we want to throw up our arms in frustration: 'Why doesn't he do something? He is making everyone's life a misery.' Until the *kairos* comes all heroic attempts by the ego to sort things out will be choked to death on the briers. For the counsellor great humility is needed. Often the counsellor's work is to 'hold' a person in distress; to be alongside them, to wait with them until the soul work is done. In Christian mysticism we find the phrase 'the dark night of the soul'. On the surface, at an ego level, it seems that nothing is happening, but deep within the psyche the soul is being made. When the spell lifts, we see that something has changed. The person is different; their personality has more depth; they are more compassionate; they have become wiser. This new life is symbolized by the marriage in the fairy tale.

Fairy tales bear on our individual stories in that they exhibit (arche)typical patterns of the psyche. Dreams, however, put us in touch with archetypes in the context of our personal lives. Dreams can be for many of us an important part of working with the shadow, for as Jung said: 'The dream is specifically the utterance of the unconscious.'[2] Interpreting dreams is, however, something of a lost art. In earlier times dreams were taken very seriously, as we have already noted, but, as we have also seen, the Apollonian commitment to reason has relegated dream interpretation to the realm of mere subjective superstition. Freud and Jung both have done much to recover this lost art for us but I believe we are very much novices here. Indeed, these pioneers of the psyche themselves showed fairly major disagreements about how dreams should be interpreted. We cautiously look to Jung's approach, less dogmatic than Freud's, to help us on our way. It may be helpful to clarify Jung's approach by comparing and contrasting Jung with Freud on the main points.[3]

Freud believed that dreams need careful decoding because they bear potentially deceptive messages. Jung, however, said: 'I take the dream for what it is . . . . The dream is a natural occurrence and there is no earthly reason why we should assume it is a crafty device to lead us astray.'⁴ The practical implication here is that we are not totally dependent on the expert psychologist to help us with our interpretations. Jung himself aimed to help his 'patients' learn how to '. . . consult the unconscious without the doctor's help.'⁵

Freud believed that dream images refer to people and places in the outer world. Jung believed that dream images refer mostly to our inner life.

Freud believed that dreams are mainly to do with fantasy fulfilment of suppressed wishes. Jung felt that this was too restrictive. He wanted to remain open to any number of meanings a dream may have.

Freud looked to dreams for the past cause of a neurosis. Jung looked to dreams to tell us which way we should go in the future. Since, according to Jung, the dream is 'a spontaneous self-portrayal, in symbolic form, of the actual situation in the unconscious', it reveals to us something that lies in the shadows.⁶ If we are ready to learn, the dream will tell us how we may integrate what is in the shadow into our conscious life.

As we know, whatever is not brought out into the light of conscious life lies in the shadow. It follows from this that dream interpretation cannot take place in a one-sided way. We need to know what is going on in conscious life in order to know what the dream is telling us from the shadows. Jung puts it like this: 'It is always helpful, when we set out to interpret a dream, to ask: What conscious attitude does it compensate?'⁷ According to Jung, then, what lies in the shadows is in a compensatory relationship to what is lived out in conscious life. Practically this means that we cannot interpret our own or anyone else's dream unless we know at a deeply empathic level what the conscious life situation of the dreamer is. Sometimes, people of whom I have little knowledge recount a dream and ask how it should be interpreted. This is a virtually impossible request.

In dream interpretation then, as the metaphor of the psychic committee similarly tries to grasp, the dynamic relationship between the ego and the shadow is crucial. This fact should alert us to two important pitfalls in dealing with dreams. The first is to do with superstition. Many people are very wary of interpreting dreams. They fear that we enter into the realm of superstition and the occult. Following Jung, interpreting dreams is not about superstition. We do not cower before the dream as though it has some mysterious occult power over us. Rather, dream interpretation involves critical assessment by the ego. We mentioned earlier the dream of the Christian apostle Peter. I feel sure that he and very probably the other apostles critically debated the meaning of the dream before they agreed on a final interpretation. This approach is consistent with what we know about 'the Wisdom from above', which is always open to reason.

The second pitfall is related to the first. We should be wary of engaging the world of dreams if our ego is unseated from the chairperson's chair, so to speak. Then we run the risk of being fascinated and even terrified by dream images. Especially if we are experiencing psychosis we should be wary of the allure of dreams. One man I worked with was particularly terrified by his dreams. He was becoming obsessed with their meaning as though his very life depended upon getting it right. I felt that first we should work on getting his ego more firmly seated before we spent time on his dreams.

Following the above guidelines, and by way of example, I will describe how I have gone about interpreting some of my own dreams from a Jungian perspective. I have in the past few years on many occasions had dreams of being driven in a car. The driver is always a female figure. A vehicle such as a car is widely accepted as an archetypal symbol for the movement of the consciousness through life. This series of dreams was very revealing. It alerted me to the fact that my ego was not in the 'driving seat' of my life but rather I was being unconsciously 'driven' by an archetypal feminine power – an 'anima' figure, as Jung called it. To refer back to the committee metaphor, the dream was telling me that a female committee member was in the chair where my ego should be. In my conscious, waking life I went about as though I was in charge of my life. My dream was compensating for this conscious attitude.

After interpreting the dream I became very conscious of how, frequently, I was at the mercy of some of the women I knew. I neurotically often needed their approval and feared their criticism. I unconsciously projected on to them my own 'driving' anima, and from their faces saw it staring back at me. I remember one particular dream in which the car, driven again by a female figure, was careering dangerously all over the road. I woke up just as it was about to crash into a brick wall. I believe this dream was telling me in no uncertain terms that I had better do some shadow work before my conscious life really did 'crash'!

Another dream I had, still on the theme of the anima, led to a particularly startling revelation for me. I should say that what follows is rare, in my life anyway. Yet it illustrates some of the points we made above for dream interpretation. The setting of my dream was a stately home and garden beyond which were wild and rugged hills. The weather was stormy and brooding. It was half light, dusk or dawn. My dream began with a young woman in a car. I recognized this young woman. In waking life she was a friend of mine. In the dream she was trying to park the car and was careering backwards and forwards. Suddenly the car transformed itself into a magnificent powerful black stallion. The young woman was riding the stallion bareback. She was naked with long flowing hair. She stopped the stallion some way off, looked at me as if to ask me if I would come with her, then turned and rode off into the hills. I was standing with her husband watching this scene. I remember feeling the urge to go with her but felt constrained by the presence of her husband.

I interpreted the dream as follows: firstly, I took the dream figures to be images of my inner life and not my outer life. There was no suggestion that the dream was tempting me to run off with my friend! My friend in real life is an artist whose work I find very alluring. It has a kind of wild, untamed quality to it. I guessed that was why my unconscious had 'chosen' her as a symbol. I believe that she was symbolic of a part of myself that was in the shadows. A part that I was not living out in my conscious life. She represented something wild, untamed, erotic, free and playful. The stallion also had this kind of quality. It was animal, instinctual, beautiful and powerful. These symbols contrasted with the other dream symbols of the house and husband. These represented for me domesticity and tameness. They lacked vitality and power – all the things symbolized by the horse and rider. I noted that in this dream I was not being driven by this female anima figure, so the dream was not explicitly inviting me to consider who was driving my life. Rather, it was inviting me to move away from the mundane, lacklustre pattern of life I had fallen into and to engage with something powerful, wild, instinctual and free in myself.

I believed the dream was particularly significant for me, given the context of my life at the time. I was yet to find out just how significant. Some time after the dream and my initial analysis of it I went on a weekend printmaking course for beginners run by a friend of mine. He asked us to choose a subject for our print. I decided on my dream image, my Anima Picture.

Several days later, I happened to show my print to another friend of mine. She said she could see another

Anima picture

figure in my dream. Like one of those gestalt perception teasers, as I stared at the picture, another feminine figure loomed hugely at the back of the stallion. She has the appearance of a dominating matriarchal figure against which the stallion and rider are severely diminished in stature. When I saw it I recognized it immediately. I have known for a long time that I have not yet fully got free from the maternal swamp we talked about earlier in the book. My picture once more brought this home to me in such an unexpected and surprising way. It told me that before I could engage with the free, powerful, instinctual energy within myself I would have to deal with this archetypal mother who still dominated my psyche. I realize that even as I write this I have invoked some painful feelings in myself. I am aware I have to do more soul work here.

What are we to make of this dream picture? Is it a mere coincidence? Or is it a fascinating way in which the unconscious can make itself known? It does, I think illustrate the point that I made earlier that in working with the shadow there are no strict guidelines we can follow. We must always be open to surprises.

8 *The Sacred Canopy*

Jung believed that for the kind of work we have been discussing in this book belief in God is crucial.[1] Dancing with the shadow takes place not in a ballroom but under a sacred canopy – of God's love. In this final part of the book I hope to show that this is not a pious platitude. To do this I want to draw from the insight of the great medieval theologian and monk Abelard. Many of us will know of him from the story of Abelard and his young student Heloise, one of the great tragic love stories. Theological students will know of Abelard for his work on the atonement. They will have learned of Abelard's moral exemplary theory of the atonement. Essentially, this states that Christ shows us the greatness of God's love for us in his life and death on the cross. We are moved by this love to go and do likewise. Students of the atonement tend to pass over Abelard's 'theory' too quickly, in my view, dismissing it as too subjective. In doing so they miss the significance of his core insight. Abelard believed that Christ 'excites in us' the love of God. This is a great psychological and theological insight. In order to dance with the shadow we need to have the love of God excited within us, as we shall see.

In Scripture and Christian tradition, a number of what we may call archetypal images are used to convey the significance of Christ, or, rather, God in Christ. Among these are 'prophet', 'priest', 'king' and 'warrior'. The love of God is mediated to us through these archetypes. Let us first think of the image 'king'. As we have seen, this is mainly about political rule, power and authority. The psychological component of the symbol of the king is about rule and power in the psyche. When we say or confess with conviction that Christ is king, we are saying that he is the one who has ultimate power. He is the one to whom 'every knee shall bow' (Phil. 2.10). God put 'everything in subjection under his feet', leaving nothing outside his control (Heb. 2.8). We see this demonstrated in Jesus' life, for example in his stilling of the storm. The disciples were amazed. They probably sensed that they were in the presence of the Creator God, of whom the Psalmist said:

> He sends forth his command to the earth . . .
> He gives snow like wool;
> he scatters hoarfrost like ashes . . .
> he makes his wind blow, and the waters flow.
> (Ps. 147.15ff.)

'Even wind and water . . . obey him'. (Luke 8.25) The disciples had touched the holiness of God, the Creator himself, who excites in us awe, fear, fascination and worship. In his casting out of demons and healing diseases, Jesus was not like the others; he spoke with authority. It is this same Jesus who with ultimate kingly power and authority 'sets the prisoners free . . . opens the eyes of the blind . . . lifts up those who are bowed down' (Ps. 146.7ff.). It is God as king of whom the Psalmist can be sure:

> If I ascend to heaven, thou art there!
>   If I make my bed in Sheol, thou art there!
> If I take the wings of the morning
>   and dwell in the uttermost parts of the sea,
> even there thy hand shall lead me,
>   and thy right hand hold me. (Ps. 139.8ff.)

If God in Christ is king, no one and nothing else can claim this authority, no 'committee member', not Aphrodite, not Hera, not Apollo. This is fundamental in working with the shadow. So often when we become aware of our shadow we despair of ever being free of the feeling or mood that holds us in its grip. It seems omnipotent. At times like this we need the authority of God excited within us. Only when the roots of our ego go down into and are nourished by this ultimate power will it have the authority to put our shadow characters in their place.

When we feel as though we are impaled on the horns of an impossible dilemma then, too, we need divine, revitalizing kingly power. The married man caught between two women believed he was doomed. Tormented by both Hera and Aphrodite, he felt that one way led to a life of never-ending guilt, the other way to a life of never-ending regret. But if Christ is king, then Hera or Aphrodite are not. This man needed to have Christ's kingship excited in him. This would lead him to realize that whichever way he goes *ultimately* all things will be well. Only then will he be able to make a robust, authentic decision, free from the tyrannical fear that if he takes the wrong path it will ultimately ruin everyone's life.

I once worked with a young woman who had very low self-esteem. This was beginning to show itself in her body. Her head hung low. Her shoulders arched over. She had no sense of inner authority. Especially at her place of work she felt that everyone was better than her, none of her opinions counted, she was dull and boring. As you can imagine she was very depressed. I asked her if there was anywhere where she felt empowered, any time that she felt like a queen. She said yes, when she was cycling. She was a keen cyclist and belonged to a cycling club. We talked about her royal realm and how small it was: the physical boundaries extended only so far as a bicycle saddle! I asked her how her armies were. Rulers and kingdoms need warriors. Warriors defend the realm and capture new territory. She said that they were pretty demoralized. I suggested that in her imagination she pay a royal visit to inspect and encourage her warriors. We even talked, half-jokingly, about the possibility of her cycling around her office!

In his letter to the Christians living at Ephesus, the apostle Paul uses the warrior metaphor. He bids them 'be strong in the Lord and in the strength of his might'. He goes on to develop this metaphor extensively, referring to all the parts of a soldier's armament. I find his reference to the sword particularly striking. Swords are weapons which cut and kill. Paul talks about the sword of the Spirit. This is a very dramatic metaphor. It is not tame. So often we seem to tame the Holy Spirit. Here the Holy Spirit is a warrior. Paul identifies the sword of the spirit with the kingly word of God, thus underlining the ultimate authority that this sword has. In shadow work we need the warrior's sword of the Spirit excited in us. We need the warrior's courage and even ruthlessness to take decisive steps forward and to gain new territory, to fight off the shadows that claim omnipotence and try to get us in their grip, and to cut the cord which ties us to old emotional patterns.

There was a lame man that Jesus happened on once (John 5.6). He asked him if he wanted to be healed, a strange question, we may think. But it is a very serious question. This story has important implications for shadow work. There is most often some pay-off or benefit for us to be caught in the grip of the shadow. Very often we are terrified by the responsibility that freedom gives us. While we stay in the grip of the one who is scared to step out, we can go on letting others take the responsibility. If we stay in the grip of 'mother', we will not have to grow up and make decisions for ourselves. Like perhaps the lame man sometimes our neurosis is our very identity. We think that it is who we are. Who would we be if we were healed? At such times we need the warrior's sword to cut us free.

I find part of the Old Testament story of David and Bathsheba particularly illuminating, or shall we say 'exciting', of warrior power. King David had (mis)used his kingly authority. He had committed a monstrous offence, one more heinous than most of us come near to committing. Moved by his erotic desire for Bathsheba, he had orchestrated the death of her husband on the battle field so that he could 'have' her. She became pregnant and a child was born. The prophet Nathan revealed to David the extent of his crime and told him that the child would die. Alone, David pleaded with God that it should not be so. He lay on the ground. He did not eat for a week. He was inconsolable. The child died, and the servants were terrified. If David was in such a state when the child was alive what would he do on hearing that the child was dead? David guessed that the child had died. The text reads:

> Then David arose from the earth, and washed, and anointed himself, and changed his clothes; and he went into the house of the Lord, and worshipped; he then went to his own house; and when he asked, they set food before him, and he ate . . . . Then David comforted his wife, Bathsheba, and went in to her, and lay with her; and she bore a son, and he called his name Solomon. And the Lord loved him . . . (2 Sam. 12.20ff.).

After becoming fully aware of the enormity of David's offence – his breaking of the commandments – we note his remorse. The way of the warrior is not by bullying suppression of feelings. The warrior engages deeply with feelings. But note David's behaviour on hearing of the child's death. Put simply, he puts it all behind him and gets on with life. He does not forever hold on to his guilt and remorse. He takes the warrior's sword and cuts. He even 'lies' with Bathsheba again! A child is born and God loves this child. The child is given the name Jedediah, meaning 'beloved of the Lord'. So often we will not allow ourselves to be forgiven – no by others, not by ourselves, not by God.

In order to move on in life we need the sword of the Spirit and the ultimate authority of the warrior king. Moving on always involves decision. 'Decision' is a warrior word. It comes from the Latin *caedere*. *Caedere* means 'to slay', as with a sword. Compare 'suicide', which means to kill oneself, or 'homicide', which means to kill a man. 'Decide' means cutting off one course of action in order to live out the other. Without the divine warrior's sword, we may find ourselves like Lot's wife, who kept looking back: our tears turn us into a pillar of salt.

Shadow work requires a prophetic spirit. This involves consciousness and judgement. Dancing with the shadow is, as we have seen, a call to consciousness. We very easily get into the grip of psychic sloth. We are pushed around by powers that are deep within our unconscious. Yet there is a great inertia which makes it difficult to get free. The beginning of getting free is becoming conscious of what it is that is running us from the depths. Dealing with this is prophecy in the psychic dimension of life. In the social dimension, the prophets of the Old Testament called the people of Israel to consciousness when they had fallen into a way of life that was morally, politically and religiously destructive. We need the prophetic spirit to call us out of a life that is destructive of the soul. The prophetic spirit is also a spirit of judgement. While we disown our shadows and project them on to others, while we go around with a beam in our own eye we need the prophetic spirit of self-judgement that calls us to engage with our shadows.

Christ as priest deals with guilt. Guilt is an enemy that lurks outside our borders. It waits to find the smallest crack in our defences. Then it worms its way in, when the king has his back turned and the warriors are engaged in some other battle. We find too late that there has been a complete take-over. Guilt makes us feel vulnerable and defenceless. All our boundaries are down. We cower in the corner. Just a word or a look from someone is like another arrow that hits us. There are two kinds of guilt. One kind has a theological focus. This guilt is part of the human condition. 'All have sinned and fall short of the glory of God,' says the apostle Paul (Rom. 3.23). In the religion of the Old Testament this kind of guilt was dealt with by the priest who offered sacrifices on behalf of the people to atone for their sin. The writer of the letter to the Hebrews tells us that Christ is both the priest who represents God's people and also the perfect sacrifice. Since he is the perfect sacrifice, he is also the ultimate sacrifice – the one who ends all sacrifice. On the cross of Christ, atonement was made finally and completely. The problem is, many of us carry a feeling of guilt in our souls, making it hard for us to fully embrace this great theological truth.

A young man I saw for a while came to counselling tormented by whether he had committed the one unforgivable sin – the sin against the Holy Spirit mentioned in the New Testament (Matt. 12.31–2). His guilt ate away at him and often paralysed him into indecision, so terrified was he of God's wrath if he should get it wrong. In the course of counselling we began to uncover many times when he had felt humiliated and shamed by his mother as a child. He had projected this child's feeling of guilt on to God. No matter how many people told him that Christ has atoned for his sin, the legacy of guilt from childhood now residing in his soul wormed its way into the crack opened up by that phrase 'the unforgivable sin against the Holy Spirit'. This young man needed to have 'excited' within his soul 'Christ the final sacrifice who has atoned for all our sin'. Many of us are terrified to be without guilt. We would feel guilty if we did not feel guilty! Close behind Christ the priest we need Christ the warrior with the sword of the Spirit to guard against our falling into such a trap.

Finally, we need to know that Christ the king, the warrior, the prophet and the priest is Christ who mediates to us the God of compassion. If we do not have compassion, we do not have Christ at all, but a pretender. Nor, we may point out, is compassion weak, as so many think: compassion is mediated through king, warrior, prophet and priest. But a king without compassion is a tyrant – an Apollonian king. Those who are in the grip of such a one insist that everything can be solved by moral, legalistic and doctrinal conformity.

A warrior without compassion is brutal and bullying with herself and with others. Like a surgeon who wants to cure everything with radical surgery the warrior without compassion wants to make great changes in life – now! Compassion teaches the warrior to wait for the *kairos*.

A prophet without compassion is unable to move on from judgement to hope. He will be unable to say, as Isaiah did:

> O afflicted one, storm-tossed, and not comforted,
> behold, I will set your stones in antimony,
> and lay your foundations with sapphires.
> I will make your pinnacles of agate,
> your gates of garnets,
> and all your walls of precious stones. (Is. 54.11–12)

A priest without compassion simply will not let guilt go.

Without compassion we will never begin to dance with the shadow. For dancing with the shadow takes place not in a ballroom but on the lap of God under the sacred canopy of the affirming, embracing arms of God.

Epilogue

Life is both a gift and a call. We are unique, individual selves – that is our gift. Our call is to discover, nurture, and live out this gift – fully: for 'the glory of God is humanity fully alive', to echo the words of Irenaeus quoted earlier. This call is also a responsibility. We may prefer to remain only partly alive and leave much of our great gift in the shadows. Or we may dance with our shadow. To dance with the shadow, under the sacred canopy of the love of God, takes courage – the courage to be who we are. As we have seen, dancing with the shadow may involve us in facing painful feelings that we long ago tried to bury. It may involve us in breaking the taboos of our community and culture: the pull to conform is great, for it is easy to live with those who conform. The Christian gospel, however, calls us to love those who do not conform; a much more courageous yet much more real and rewarding task. Dancing with our shadow calls us to live courageously with, and out of, the wounds, failures and disappointments in our lives, knowing that these too are part of the gift of who we are.

Yet, our individual gifted selves are not isolated selves, but selves in community with each other. Dancing with our shadow is not self-centred. When we dance with our shadow, we are less likely to project our own distorting and destructive images on to others or on to God. We are also more in touch with, yet less dominated by, the archetypal energies that, in their proper place are foundational for community.

When we dance with our shadow we are more fully alive to God, each other, our world and ourselves in all dimensions of our lives together. In our moral life we are less threatened and therefore more able to trust each other with the deepest things of our souls. In the political dimension of our lives we are less paralysed, more concerned and empowered to do justice when we see injustice. In our faith-life we are stronger and more secure, knowing more fully the height and the depth of the love of God. In the economic dimension of our lives we are more able to take up the warrior's sword to make decisions and take responsibility for the resources God has entrusted to us; in our social lives we are more sure of ourselves, therefore more able to treat each other with dignity and respect.

When we dance with our shadow we dance with Sophia. She brings imagination, discovery and playfulness. Thus we bring more joy to others.

When we dance with our shadow, we cease from forcing people and ourselves into narrow, marginalizing, conceptual boxes. We let ourselves be the gifted individuals we all are. We are also less oppressively moralistic and judgemental and more concerned with liberating the oppressed. Dancing with our shadow is being closer to the heart of the Christian gospel.

Dancing with our shadow calls for us to rediscover a lost art – of engaging with those parts of our gifted selves that stir in the deepest shadows of the forgotten soul. I hope that in these pages I have helped a few of us to step on to the dance floor.

Notes

Chapter 1

1 Jung also used the term 'shadow' to mean the 'collective unconscious'. We will explore the concept of the collective unconscious in chapter 3 of this book.

Chapter 2

1 I have explored more fully the doctrine of creation and its implications for the mediated presence of God in *No Splits* (Marshall Pickering 1989).
2 Von Rad, G., *Old Testament Theology*, vol. 1 (SCM Press 1975), p. 422.
3 Scobie, C., 'The Place of Wisdom in Biblical Theology', *Biblical Theology Bulletin*, vol. XIV (April 1984), p. 46.
4 Caputo, J.D., *Radical Hermeneutics* (Indiana University Press 1987), p. 258.

Chapter 3

1 Miller, A., *The Drama of Being a Child* (Virago Press 1987), p. 27.
2 Montague, A., *Touching* (Harper & Row 1971), p. 189.
3 Bly, R., *Iron John* (Element Books 1992), pp. 92ff.
4 Barr, J., 'Abba Isn't Daddy', *Journal of Theological Studies*, vol. 39 (1988), pp. 28–47.
5 Boswell, J., *Christianity, Social Tolerance and Homosexuality* (University of Chicago Press 1980).
6 Masson, J., *Against Therapy* (Collins 1989), pp. 39ff.
7 Jung, C. G., *The Archetypes and the Collective Unconscious* (Routledge & Kegan Paul 1990), p. 39.
8 Nelson, J., *The Intimate Connection* (SPCK 1992), p. 71.
9 Each of these concepts is controversial and continues to be the subject of debate among theoreticians and analysts. See Jung, *The Archetypes*, and for a full critical analysis see Samuels, A., *Jung and the Post-Jungians* (Routledge & Kegan Paul 1985).
10 Jung, *The Archetypes*, p. 39.
11 Angelou, M., *And Still I Rise* (Virago Press 1989).
12 van der Post, L., *Jung and the Story of Our Time* (Penguin 1978).
13 The term 'borderline' is confusingly also used for a specific personality disorder.

Chapter 4

1 The theological perspective on the collective shadow that I take in this chapter is mine and not Jung's. I have explored the subject of idolatry more fully in *No Splits* (Marshall Pickering 1989).

2 Fowler, J., *Stages of Faith: The Psychology of Human Development and the Quest for Meaning* (Harper & Row 1981), p. 4.

3 Tillich, P., *Dynamics of Faith* (Harper & Row 1957), p. 1.

4 Wink, W., *Unmasking the Powers* (Fortress Press 1989), p. 116.

5 Wink, *Unmasking*, p. 122.

6 Aulen, G., *Christus Victor* (SPCK 1965). Andrew Walker, in his book *Enemy Territory* (Hodder & Stoughton 1987) has more recently argued that Christianity is essentially about a dramatic battle with evil powers.

7 The New Testament theologian Morna Hooker has recently shown that the idea that Christ's death is a substitution for our own death is a misunderstanding of a number of biblical texts: Hooker, M., *Not Ashamed of the Gospel* (Paternoster Press 1994).

8 For the link between idolatry and enslavement to evil powers see Gunton, C., *Actuality of Atonement* (T. & T. Clark 1988).

9 van der Post, L., *Jung and the Story of Our Time* (Penguin 1979), p. 213.

10 Wink, *Unmasking*, p. 127.

11 Up to this point in the Genesis text Adam (literally 'earth person') includes both genders. The separation into male and female comes later at Genesis 2.21ff.

12 Plato, *Phaedo*, para. 66.

13 Moore, T., *Care of the Soul* (Harper Collins 1992).

14 Ranke-Heinemann, U., *Eunuchs for Heaven* (Andre Deutsch 1990), p. 43.

15 Griffin, S., *Pornography and Silence* (The Women's Press 1981).

16 From a conservation with James Nelson at the College House Conference, September 1994.

17 Capra, F., *The Turning Point* (Fontana 1982); Stern, K., *The Flight From Woman* (Allen & Unwin 1966), p. 76.

18 Taylor, J. V., *The Go Between God* (SCM Press 1972), pp. 50–2.
19 Otto, R., *The Idea of the Holy* (OUP 1968).
20 For a historical survey of the understanding of some of the early Fathers of the Church of the Spirit as feminine, see Soskice, J., *After Eve* (Marshall Pickering 1990).
21 Johnson, R., *Inner Work* (Harper & Row 1986), p. 10.

Chapter 5

1 I have discussed in *No Splits* (Marshall Pickering 1989) the theological issues around self-centredness.
2 Wink, W., *Unmasking the Powers* (Fortress Press 1989), p. 127.

Chapter 6

1 Angelou, *And Still I Rise*.
2 Gendlin, E., *Focusing* (Bantam Books 1981), p. 44.
3 Gendlin, *Focusing*, p. 44
4 Johnson, R., *Owning Your Own Shadow* (HarperCollins 1991), pp. 64–5.

Chapter 7

1 A Freudian interpretation of this part of the tale majors ex-clusively on the sexual component: puberty, pricking the finger and (menstrual) blood. Jung fell out with Freud over the sexual issue. Freud believed that sex was the primary instinct. Jung believed that this was a reductionism on Freud's part that betrayed a religious allegiance. See Jung, C. G., *Memories, Dreams, Reflections* (Collins 1961), pp. 174ff.
2 Jung, C. G., *Modern Man in Search of a Soul* (Ark 1984), p. 13.
3 I refer the interested reader to Andrew Samuels' book *Jung and the Post-Jungians* (Routledge & Kegan Paul 1985) for a survey of the two positions.
4 Samuels, *Jung and the Post-Jungians*, p. 230.
5 Jung, *Modern Man*, p. 16.
6 Samuels, *Jung and the Post-Jungians*, p. 231.
7 Jung, *Modern Man*, p. 20.

Chapter 8

1 See, for example, Anthony Storr in *Jung: Selected Writings* (Fontana 1983), p. 238.

Selected Bibliography

The following is a selection of books that I have found particularly helpful and accessible on Jung and various aspects of his thought.

Introduction to Jung's Thought

Fordham, F., *An Introduction to Jung's Psychology* (Pelican 1986).
Storr, A., *Jung* (Fontana 1973).

Critical Works on Jung's Thought

Masson, J., *Against Therapy* (Collins 1989).
Samuels, A., *Jung and the Post-Jungians* (Routledge & Kegan Paul 1985).

Biographical

van der Post, L., *Jung and the Story of Our Time* (Penguin 1978).

By Jung

Autobiographical:
Jung, C. G., *Memories, Dreams, Reflections* (Collins 1961).
Jung, C. G., *Collected Works of C. G. Jung.* Translated by R. F. C. Hull (Princeton University Press 1972). Many parts have been published as paperbacks. I have found the following particularly useful:
Jung C. G., *Modern Man in Search of a Soul* (Ark 1984).
— *The Archetypes and the Collective Unconscious* (Routledge and Kegan Paul 1980).

Christian Approaches to Jung

Bryant, C., *Depth Psychology and Religious Belief* (Darton, Longman & Todd 1987).
— *Jung and the Christian Way* (Darton, Longman & Todd 1983).
Kelsey, M., *Christo-Psychology* (Darton, Longman & Todd 1983).

Jung and Feminism

Wehr, D. S., *Jung and Feminism* (Routledge & Kegan Paul 1988).

Jung and Religion

Stein, R. and Moore, R. L. (eds), *Jung's Challenge to Contemporary Religion* (Chiron 1987).

Popular Books by Jungians

Jacoby, M., *Witches, Ogres, and the Devil's Daughter: Encounters with Evil in Fairy Tales* (Shambhala 1992).
Johnson, R. A., *Inner Work* (Harper & Row 1986).
— *Owning Your Own Shadow* (HarperCollins 1991).
Moore, T., *Care of the Soul* (HarperCollins 1992).
Von Franz, M. L., *The Feminine in Fairy Tales* (Shambhala 1993).
Woodman, M., *Leaving My Father's House: A Journey to Conscious Femininity* (Rider 1993).